My Body is a Fu$king Masterpiece

Learning to love your body as it is.
Plus, other self-love practices

From your friend who gets it.

Dani Begley

Copyright © 2024 by Dani Begley

ISBN: 9798218481872

To anyone who has felt like their body is the problem.

Who has felt unworthy.

Felt less than.

This is for you.

I see you, and you are enough.

Where this all began

A month before my 29th birthday, I woke up in a house I would only end up renting for a month, newly single. My two biggest concerns were whether I could pay all the bills alone and more importantly, would I be single for the rest of my life. You see, my boyfriend had recently dumped me from a nearly 6-year relationship. We had lived together and created a home; I thought we had become a family. But after some time of him not coming home until late hours and not responding to my texts or calls, I finally asked him what the fuck was going on. I INITIATED OUR BREAK UP. Yep, he was too much of a coward. In hindsight, I'm not sure what I was more pissed about, the fact he wanted to break up with me or the fact he was too much of a pussy to do it without me calling him out. Oh, did I mention I had already forgiven him for cheating on me once before? Yeah, I was a mess.

I never had planned for this to happen. I always envisioned myself married before age 30 with a kid or close to having a kid. I blame all the years of playing MASH (iykyk) I was destined to be married and live in a mansion with a few kids and a shit ton of money. *Hello,* why was that game not fact? Not to mention, in the midst of this relationship, my dad was diagnosed with early-stage Alzheimer's. *Ugh.* Being a daddy's girl, I desperately wanted him to walk me down the aisle, give me away at my wedding, and have a father/daughter dance. The idea of not being able to have that—unless I took it to the next step with my ex—made me ready to fast-track the relationship, despite knowing in my gut it was ALL WRONG. I was living a life I thought I *should* be living, but it felt fucking awful. I was willing to stick with it because I had spent years with this man and thought there was no way someone else would want to be with me. I hated myself. I hated my body. I was miserable as me. I didn't realize it then, but looking back, it was so obvious. I went back and forth between binge eating, emotional eating/drinking, and insane restriction. I was obsessed with my appearance and constantly self-conscious and thought I could only be loved if I was beautiful and thin. I even thought that I *deserved* to be cheated on because I had "let myself go." I was ugly and disgusting, and therefore, I should have been cheated on. My fault. *WHAT THE FUCK?!*

I left that relationship with zero idea of who I was, what I liked, wanted, or what brought me joy. I hated everything about what I saw in the mirror; even if people told me I was beautiful, I didn't believe it. I had lost myself, period. This experience was a horrible time in my life, but I'm SO THANKFUL it happened. (*SAY WHAT?!*) This was the catalyst I needed in order to learn to love myself for who I am. I learned to do what makes me happy, brings me joy, and FUCK ALL THE OTHER NOISE. During this awkward phase, I developed the practices I will share in this book, and my confidence began to shine! Ultimately, I learned that finding yourself is a journey. It is never-ending, it is twisty-turny, and ever-evolving. If you're ready for that roller coaster, you are in the right place.

Buckle up, beautiful; let's get to work.

PS. I hope you're not opposed to profanity. I'd like to say I'm trying to quit, but I'm not going to start our relationship with a lie. You've been warned. Sometimes, it's just necessary to emphasize the point, ya know?

Oh, the places we are going to go!

If you're a planner or curious by nature, here is your roadmap to what to expect on this journey.

Section I : The Past Doesn't Always Stay In The Past   10

Chapter 1: So You Were Called Fat; Now What?   13

Chapter 2: Body Baggage   31

Chapter 3: Diet Demise   43

Chapter 4: Dating, Patterns, And The Patriarchy   57

Chapter 5: Comparison And Societal Bullshit   71

Section II: Getting To Know Yourself + Strengthening Your

Self-Love And Confidence Muscles.   83

Chapter 6: Who The Hell Am I?   85

Chapter 7: Feeling The Feelings   97

Chapter 8: Busting Through Your Comfort Zone   113

Chapter 9: Keeping Promises To Yourself   127

Chapter 10: The Subtle Art Of Saying No   137

Section III: The Life-Changing Art Of Gratitude, Plus Other Practices To Improve Your Life 147

Chapter 11: Cultivating A Gratitude Practice And Writing Shit Down 149

Chapter 12: Move Ya Body, Girl… (Make The Fellas Go) 163

Chapter 13: Personal Development And The Art Of Cultivating A Morning Routine 173

Chapter 14: BBBE Boundaries And Bad Bitch Energy 185

Chapter 15: When All Else Fails, Breathe. 199

Acknowledgements 219

Section I

The past doesn't always stay in the past.

Chapter 1

So you were called fat; now what?

Several memories are seared into my brain from childhood that were the catalyst to my becoming aware of my body and how it *apparently* was all wrong. Looking back, I've often wondered if everyone has an instance in their life that makes them begin to have awareness of their body and what other people think of it. At some point in our existence, we go from being carefree kids running around without concern about what others think of our body, our personality, our appearance, our intelligence, and what we eat or don't eat; to being hyper aware of others opinions. When I see little kids running around on the beach with their little bellies hanging out, sitting down, and playing in the sand, they have the biggest smiles on their faces; they aren't worried about what any person is thinking of them for one second. Their goal is building that sand castle, digging up a seashell, or jumping through the waves. Women, however, from teens to adults, are not nearly as carefree. You can see they are conscious of their bodies and what their peers and strangers may think of them. They aren't as inclined to be running around the beach because their bodies are surely going to bounce around in an unflattering way and cellulite will be on full display. Sitting hunched over digging up a seashell or making a sand castle, God forbid the possibility of their stomach folding over in a horrifically bad angle. Hell, so many women don't even take their cover-ups off because of their body insecurity. I find so curious this stark change in body consciousness, and I realized that several instances changed my perception of myself and caused my body obsession. I know I'm not alone in these situations, so let's dive in.

As a kid, I was really tall for my age. I had what seemed like the first growth spurt of anyone else in my class, and I towered over most of my peers, especially all the boys. Seriously, I was a good six inches taller than most of my classmates in kindergarten. Yes, kindergarten. It was wild. I also was a little chunky, but I was cute. I had dark curly hair and big dimples; honestly, I was adorable. At that time, I didn't have any sense of awareness that the fact that I looked a little different would be a cause for concern. I was happy playing sports with my dad, swimming in our pool, dancing, singing, and performing to any audience that would have me. I wanted to be the center of attention, and I commanded it; the idea of feeling insecure didn't exist in my world. My poor younger brother could never have any pictures without me in them because, *hello, look at me, I have to be part of this*! Sorry, Tyler.

One day, I was walking home from school. I was 9 years old. My friend and I were busy living in our very important third-grade world when two older boys approached us. Immediately, I felt uncomfortable; 9-year-old gut intuition was already kicking in. I had seen these boys around and knew they were bad news. I just wanted to keep walking and act like they didn't exist, but that was clearly not their agenda. Isn't it funny how, even at that age, *some men* just can't deal with being ignored by the opposite sex? They proceeded to say, "Hey, aren't you (me) the fat girl that walks to school with her skinny friend (my friend)?"

My heart dropped. I didn't know the reason why, but I knew that being called fat was one of the worst things to be called. My cheeks became bright red, my heart was beating in a way I thought would beat right out of my chest, and the tears, oh boy, I could feel them welling up in my eyes, but I did NOT want these boys to see me cry. I kept walking and said, "I don't know what you're talking about." My friend tried defending me, saying I wasn't fat and we weren't those girls—we knew who they were referring to, and it wasn't us! We finally got them to stop harassing us, and once they were gone, the tears flooded out of my eyes, and I could barely breathe. I was torn between wanting to rush home and staying away because I did not want to tell anyone what happened. When it came time to tell our parents, let me tell you, I was so ashamed. I was embarrassed that not only did these dumb boys know I was fat, but now my parents and my friend's parents also knew I was fat, or if they hadn't already thought I was fat, they were thinking it now. It got worse. Our parents told our teachers, so I had to relive the shame again.

As a 9-year-old, I was already embarrassed by my body. I didn't really know why, but I knew that how I looked had caused all of this drama, and for that reason, I began hating my body. It would be very soon after this event that I started all the countless ways of trying to shrink my body, ways of punishing my body, and ultimately, the obsession with food, body image, and self-hatred. At 9 years old, I should have been carefree, but I was not.

I wish I could say this was my only instance of being called fat, but it would be one of many. Sometimes, it wasn't so blatant; in fact, often, it was backhanded compliments, you know the kind. Like a sweet little lady with a thick southern accent, "Bless your heart, sweetie, you sure do have a cute face at least!" or, "My heavens, you're so beautiful darling, if you'd just lose some weight, you'd be a knockout!". It's funny, now that I'm older, I'd almost rather someone just call me fat without all the pomp and circumstance. All these compliments do is teach us that our worth, our place in this world, and our values are based not just on our face and its beauty but, even more importantly, our thinness. It's as if it is a shame to waste a pretty face on a fat body. This idea kept being drilled into my head over and over.

That first instance of being called fat heightened my awareness, and I started paying attention to every comment, every side eye, every extended glance, and every tone of voice. I would walk into a room and quickly assess if there happened to be anyone who was fatter than me. Somehow, that would bring some sort of weird peace, knowing I wasn't the biggest person there. Many times, though, I would be the biggest person in the room, and that is when the anxiety kicked in, long before I had any idea what anxiety was. Those times, I felt like I couldn't take a deep breath. I had to suck in my body as much as possible, barely make a move, and ensure I would not draw any attention to myself. At this time, I also became very aware of my clothes and how they fit. If they began to get too small, I would freak out. Once, when shopping for school clothes, I remember vividly my mom getting annoyed at how my clothes didn't fit, and we had to go get bigger sizes. Yet another instance of shame, guilt, and burying my emotions. After all, what could I say? My body was clearly the problem, but I had no idea what to do about it.

I loved dancing growing up—not as much as sports— but I loved expressing myself and was fortunate enough to try many types of dance. Looking back, I realize that my body was definitely different from that of my peers, but I was happy and didn't notice. That all changed after the incident with those boys; now I was grossly aware of my size and how I always had to look for the largest size shirt or, God forbid, get an adult size. I remember the last dance class I took was with a group of my friends, and it should have been fun, but when it came to the costumes—the leotards—the studio didn't have a size that would fit me. I wished I could have vanished right then and there. I was mortified that they had to order a special size for me. Looking back, it's so insane to me because it's not as if I was 500 lbs. I was simply a tall, chunky girl about to hit puberty way earlier than her friends. Finding a leotard to fit my body shouldn't have been that difficult. Yet it was another instance seared into my brain, reinforcing what it already knew to be true: my body was the problem.

I know my family did their best, and comments were —at least I believe—unintentional, but again, my senses had become unnaturally heightened when it came to my body, food, and, now, other people's bodies and food. My grandmother is a petite woman. She's every bit of 5'1 and has probably never weighed more than 120 lbs. She is someone who will eat cookies for breakfast and an apple or orange for lunch and be fine. Cooking for others is her love language, one that she excels in. Growing up, I loved her cooking—all real ingredients, real butter, sugar, and love. Everything came with cheese, and the desserts were decadent and addicting. Weight and diets were always fair conversations at the dinner table, and I hated it. My grandmother would comment on whatever diet my grandfather was trying and how he needed to lose weight. My aunt always said this was her last meal before starting whatever new diet tomorrow. I learned that these foods, made with love, were inherently bad because if not, why would they be giving them up? My loving grandmother constantly commented on my weight. She would tell me if I had gained weight or lost weight and make comments on how I was so pretty; I just needed to lose weight, and I would be even prettier. She's not the only person I heard this from. In fact, it became so regular that it became my identity—the pretty fat girl.

What the fuck kind of identity is that? Especially when, at the time, I didn't believe I was pretty; how could I when the world made me feel less than because of my body? This identity was something I carried into adulthood, and sometimes, that voice of young Dani still creeps in. My view on fatness tainted my life for YEARS. It wasn't just the internal dialogue I had around being fat; it was the silent and unintentional bias I realized I had about other fat people. I would judge them too. WTF, right? We don't even recognize our inherent biases, believe me. But for whatever reason, all the years of sizing up the room (literally) to make sure I wasn't the fattest of them all had solidified my view of other fat people. I didn't want to do that anymore. I got to a point where I was so fed up being obsessed with the size of my body I knew it was on me to do something.

What changed?

I was utterly exhausted from the constant thought of what I should or should not be eating, the yo-yo dieting, and constantly avoiding mirrors or using them to torture myself. I also started noticing how women of every age—all the way up to 70+ years old, still seemed to constantly be discussing their distaste for their body and desire to change it. What was their recent diet plan or exercise? How they'd been so "bad" lately, etc. I thought, how fucking sad is it that all these women, who were successful in their careers, in their lives, had families, relationships, you name it, had nothing more interesting to talk about than diets and their bodies. It hit me how long I had already spent obsessing about shrinking my body—since those asshole dudes called me fat at 9 years old—and how I did not want to end up being in my 40s, 50s, or any other age, still talking about how I wanted my body to change. Life is too fucking short for that, and I was simply sick of it, I still am. Do I still, at times, feel like 9-year-old Dani, worried about my body? Yes. But now I remind myself of all the time I wasted being obsessed with making my body smaller and how I'm not letting it take any more of my time away. It's not a perfect science, but it worked. That being sick and tired of the BS feeling is reinforced every time I overhear women beating themselves up over their bodies. It's like an "aha, yep, I don't want to do that anymore" feeling.

I also realized the numerous things in my life that I wanted to do, but I held myself back for fear of rejection or negative comments about my body. I've always loved music; I took singing, piano, and guitar lessons and wrote song lyrics. Yet I've never performed in front of people- except drunken karaoke or bar bands—always with liquid courage. As I already mentioned, I loved entertaining growing up. I always wanted to audition for the musicals in high school, and I NEVER did. I was petrified of my body being on display, and my inner mean girl (I call her Barb) nearly threatened my life over the mere thought of performing as a teenager. It's actually really sad when I think about it. It's something I've always loved but never pursued because it was easier to blend in. But living your life half-assed, ignoring things you love and want to pursue for comfort and fear of rejection, is just setting yourself up for living a life not so worth living. I was fed up feeling like I was going through the motions and only half-living.

Maybe you, too, feel fed up, so sick of thinking of food and diets and comparing your bodies and always trying to make yourself be something you're not. Or you're tired of having these conversations with others; you don't want to pass down this obsession to your daughters or sons, and you want to be free. You'd like to look into the mirror and not be filled with hate. You'd like to have the freedom to go to dinner, trust yourself with food, and not worry about the calorie content or macro make up, but actually, just enjoy your meal and feel good. I hope this book can help you with that, and I hope that hearing my struggles and breakthroughs will be motivating. At the end of each chapter, I'll offer tangible, take-action tips to use in your journey. With that being said:

You were called fat—now what? Here are my tips to move past it.

1.   *Bless and release.*

If someone has called you fat, bless and release it. At the end of the day, hurt people, hurt people. People who are miserable in their lives are the ones who take pleasure in hurting others. Have you ever met a truly happy person who takes pleasure in calling women fat? Or calling someone a disgusting pig? I hope not because people who have done the healing are not putting that negativity out there. Besides, are those negative assholes the kind of people you would want in your life? If they aren't someone you would keep in your life, then who gives a fuck what they think—they don't matter to you. Holding on to resentment and anger doesn't help anything. Bless and release their negativity and move on with your life. I promise you'll be better for it. Wish them well and keep it moving.

2.   *Watch how you talk to yourself—Name your Mean Girl.*

If you're anything like me, you can and probably have said the most hurtful things to yourself. Things you would NEVER say to even your worst enemy. Horrible, disgusting, name-calling, bullying type of shit. Honestly, I would be embarrassed ever to say some of the things I have thought about myself out loud; they are so bad. This is why I like to name that voice in my head: the mean girl, the bully. Give her a name; mine is Barb. Sorry to all those named Barb, but it just fits me, ok? I'm sure you're thinking I'm cuckoo right about now, but stay with me. The next time you're standing in front of the mirror and you criticize your body, "Ugh, you're so fat, you're disgusting; how did you ever let yourself get this bad?" You pause and confront Barb. Tell her thanks for sharing her unwanted opinion, but she can fuck all the way off. Acknowledging that voice as an entity outside of yourself helps you disassociate from your brain and realize that what your inner mean girl is saying is not true, so your brain doesn't have to keep searching for evidence that it is. I promise it may feel weird at first, but when I can call Barb out for being on her shit, I can laugh and move forward almost instantly.

3.   *Excuse yourself from diet/negative body talk.*

I will bet you that once you read this book, you will start noticing just how much people around you talk about diets, their bodies, other people's bodies, insecurities, etc. THIS IS GOOD! Recognizing this talk will make it easier to excuse yourself from it. Yes, you will have to work on leaving those conversations. I'm not saying to be rude or to carry around an airhorn to blast anytime someone is talking about diet and body issues, but you can change the subject. If that doesn't work, you can even say, this is something I've been working on not talking about, I'd love it if we could talk about something else. Or if you're not there yet, maybe its a perfect bathroom break. Protect your energy. If you can say you don't want to discuss religion or politics, you can do the same here. I personally think negative body talk is something that should NOT be as normalized as it is.

4. *Accept yourself as you are and be grateful for your body.*

You can love your body and still want to improve it. You can be grateful for your body and still want to be stronger, leaner, or feel better. The point is, you first have to love it. Two of my favorite ways of doing this are through positive body affirmations and a gratitude practice. Some of my favorite affirmations are:

- *My body is so strong and beautiful, just as it is.*
- *My body is one of a kind, and that is what makes it so special.*
- *My body is a fucking masterpiece.*
- *I love my body, and I'm comfortable in it.*

Gratitude, for me, is a mental shift of "get to do" instead of "have to do." So it may look like, "I am so grateful for my body for how it carries me through the day." "I am so grateful I am strong enough to move my body." "I am grateful for my healthy body and all it does for me." Sometimes, we have to pause and remember that not everyone can walk, move, feel, or see. That alone is enough for me to be extra grateful for what my body can do and what it gets to do instead of what it looks like. We spend so much time putting our bodies down, and obsessing over what they are "supposedly" lacking; what if we shift that energy into all our bodies do for us? I genuinely write down often, "I am so grateful for how my body keeps me healthy and strong." What a powerful mental shift.

5. *Stop weighing and measuring yourself.*

Look, I'm not a doctor, but from my own experience, constantly weighing yourself is just not a good measurement of success. If you're like me, that number can be a mind fuck. It can be the determinant of a good or bad day. Why should a number dictate my mood? If I've been fueling my body with nutritious foods, sleeping like a baby, honoring my body through movement, and am feeling energetic, strong, and happy—-who gives a flying fuck how much I weigh? How I feel is what matters. If I've been doing all those things and then see I have gained weight—that can be just the thing to set me off on a "Fuck it" day. It's just dumb, especially as a female, because the sun and all the stars need to be aligned to see a number you want to see on a scale. I could literally go up and down 5lbs in a day, especially if I'm on my period. Measure how you feel and not what the number is. It releases the pressure and the obsession.

6. *Non-Body compliments.*

Instead of complimenting someone's figure or asking, "Did you lose weight?" or any other kind of body-related compliment, try instead a non-body compliment. "You are such a great support system to me." " You inspire me." "You are so wise on XYZ topic." "You're an amazing friend, wife, mother, etc." "Your energy is magnetic." Try it, please! I'm not saying there aren't days it feels good to have someone tell you how hot you look, but it's surface level and perpetuates the belief that our value is based on our outward appearance. Comments on who we are inherently are profound and so meaningful—why not try to sprinkle those in?

7. *Find someone who inspires you and channel their energy.*

I have said it so many times: I wonder what my teenage years would have been like if we had people in the entertainment business who were plus size or in any way representative of myself. I have a few go-to women I follow on Instagram, and anytime I'm feeling insecure or lacking confidence, I go to their page for inspiration. Lizzo is my go-to. She exudes confidence, and she doesn't GAF about what people think. I channel my inner Lizzo and remember the bad bitch I am. Find your muse.

8. *Stop hiding yourself.*

I hid for so long in baggy clothes, never wearing a 2 piece swimsuit or crop top. It took me some time, but now I rock it. After years of hiding behind all black clothes and hiding my body, I remind myself if I like the clothes, I wear them. Who cares what someone else thinks? As long as it makes me happy, that's all that matters. The amount of time I have spent trying to find an outfit that can accentuate one part of my body while minimizing another is embarrassing and always results in half my closet on the floor and me feeling horrible about my body. As hard as it is sometimes, I make it a point to wear the first thing I try on without overthinking it…what a time saver.

9. *Don't wait.*

Don't wait to lose 10lbs or until you fit into the dress to do something you really want to do. DO IT NOW. Otherwise, you'll never do it. Trust me. There will always be a reason in your head; if it's not the size or the weight, it's you and your inner Barb telling you that people are going to judge you. Guess what, sweetheart? Most people aren't even thinking about you. So take the trip, do the photoshoot, go on a date, do whatever it is you've been putting off, do it NOW!

10. *Remind yourself of the time wasted hating your body.*

When all else fails, remind yourself of just how many years you've already wasted hating your body. I feel sick sometimes when I acknowledge it. If that somehow doesn't do the trick, think about being in your 60s, 70s, 80s, or, God forbid, on your death bed and thinking of how you wish your body was smaller. ARE YOU FOR REAL? I often say when I die, no one is going to be talking at my funeral about how they miss the way my body looked or how I should have lost weight. (They better not be, or I'm going to haunt them for eternity!) Our bodies are the least interesting part of us. We are so much more than the shell in which our soul lives. Think of all your great qualities that have nothing to do with your body, write those down, and come back to them when you need a reminder. I promise you, your friends and family, the people who LOVE you, love those qualities, not the size of your jeans or the number on the scale.

My Body is a Fu$king Masterpiece

Chapter 2
Body Baggage

When I hear a woman say that she wishes she had bigger boobs, my immediate thought is, "No, you don't." Women with smaller chests always look at me like I'm crazy, but if you know, you know. When I was 11, I started to develop. If you're a woman, you know this awkward, out-of-body feeling. It's like you're an alien inside your own, now foreign body. No one prepared me for this, not health class or my mom, and I didn't have any older sisters to warn me. Not only did my monthly bleed come and freak me out, I was now the proud owner of substantial-sized boobs and was going into 6th grade looking like I was 16. *Cool.* It's been many years since I was 11, and yet I still can remember the boys in my class commenting after summer break how "Dani had the biggest boobs of all the girls." It was mortifying. It felt like I had 2 strobe lights on my chest that everyone was not only noticing but also being blinded by. I wonder if things had started out differently for the girls and me, if we would have had a better relationship over the years? I guess I'll never know. I surely empathized with Ramona from the movie Now and Then —you're not an elder millennial if you didn't watch the shit out of that movie—taping her boobs down. Back then, I was a tomboy, obsessed with playing sports, and my boobs weren't super conducive to running and jumping. So, while other girls added tissues to their bras, I understood the appeal of taping those things down.

When I look back, I see exactly why I felt that way. Yes, of course, large breasts can be uncomfortable; they are heavy, they can make you have backaches, and you feel the need to have on multiple sports bras when exercising. This is all still true to this day. But it wasn't just that; the unwanted attention they brought into my life made me resent them.

First, let me set the record straight that women with large tatas are NOT always trying to flaunt them (yes, I'm speaking to all you judgy Judys and creepy Carls out there). It just so happens that they are large and in charge, and with most styles that aren't out of the Catholic nun catalog, it's hard not to show a bit of them, even when you don't want to. Now, flaunt them if you want to, girl, sometimes it's necessary, I get it. But for a long time, I tried wearing sports bras or any other bra that wasn't a push-up, something to minimize. I made sure to wear baggy clothes with high necklines because I did not want to be showing off the girls. And I will 1000% say it was because of how I felt with the unwanted attention. Let me tell you, we know when you're staring. It's obvious despite your most valiant efforts and a sincere fuck you to the ones that don't even try to hide their creepiness.

What I would really love is if we could normalize having conversations with young women about how to become comfortable with their new womanly bodies and how to handle attention-especially from men. There is no manual on this, to my knowledge, and it's a cluster fuck. I can remember being 13 or 14 years old with the body of a woman and having men stare at my chest—not just boys my age, but grown-ass men. At that age, I could have passed for 17 or 18 years old, which is not really helpful to someone trying to be invisible. When a grown-ass man stares at you as a teenager, it's disgusting, and it feels all kinds of wrong. This is yet another reason I felt constant shame about my body. I had finally grown into it, shed some weight, and was wearing normal-sized clothes, and the attention I was receiving, I didn't know how to handle, nor did I want to.

During 8th grade, I started dating a new boy. He hadn't gone to my elementary school and hung around some of the "cool boys". This boy, let's call him Henry, was interested in me, and I was super excited. We started dating and hanging out pretty regularly. Now, back then, obviously, we didn't drive, so we watched a lot of movies, and we ended up spending a lot of time at his house. He had a finished basement where we spent ALL our time on the couch "watching movies." I had been kissed before, but they were more innocent kisses, not full-on make-out sessions. A lot of spin the bottle, truth or dare, suck and blow… those kind of games. Henry and I got really good at kissing. We took the kissing horizontal—just kissing—but it was way more advanced for my very naive 13 years. I had heard rumors that his two best friends had been doing more than kissing with their girlfriends. Assuming they were comparing notes and Henry would likely want to be on the same page, I was low-key freaking out.

A few weeks had passed, and we continued our normal routine of picking a movie to watch, only to not actually watch it—the late 90s/early 2000s version of Netflix & Chill—Blockbuster and Blue Balls. Things were good. One day, I came over to his house to find that his parents weren't home, not that it was much different, because we always went straight downstairs; in fact, I don't think I even knew what the upstairs of his house looked like. That day, he decided to show me his room, conveniently located in the basement, instead of us taking our usual position on the couch. Before I knew it, we were horizontal in his bed, entangled in a hefty make-out session. His hands started roaming in areas they never had before, starting at my waist and slowly making their way north. I kept shifting, moving, trying to avoid the inevitability of what I knew he was intending—get to second base, of course. I was either going to inflict spinal damage with all the shifting, say something, or allow it to happen. So, like a lot of young girls who don't know what the fuck they are doing, I let his hand explore the girls. It's not that it felt bad, but it didn't feel right either. I was not ready for this at thirteen years old, inside I was losing it, but I had no idea what to do or how to stop it. When his other hand started moving towards my belt buckle—looking back, I'm honestly thankful that those huge, gaudy belt buckles were the style back then— I came up for air and said I had to go to the bathroom. That was literally the only thing that came to mind, and spoiler alert—it would not be the last time I used it as an excuse to take a minute. Thank God his parents came home, and I was spared. I knew we needed to have a conversation, but I didn't know how to. Hell, 20 years later, it was still hard to have those conversations.

So what happened to Henry and me? A few weeks later, I went on vacation with my family, and when I returned, I broke up with him. He thought I met someone on vacation; naive thinking on his part. I simply told him I'd been thinking of ending it for a while and being away on vacation made me realize it was time. He was upset, honestly, so was I. My first "real" boyfriend after my 6th-grade sweetheart, Chris (honestly, I should have stayed with him, but I was dumb), and the summer before 9th grade, I knew it was the easier choice for me to end things before I had to actually say no, or worse go through with something I wasn't ready for. I was perhaps more of a people pleaser back then; actually, no doubt about it, I was. Years of being conditioned to prove my worth by good grades, doing well in sports, and being acknowledged as the sweet young lady, I learned that my value came from others' validation. Not to mention that the dichotomy of both wanting to have "some" male attention and also hating male attention, was a major mind fuck at this time.

You may wonder why I told this story when I'm talking about body baggage. Well, after doing a lot of self-reflecting and even some EDMR therapy, I realized that this was one of those moments that, in a way other than being fat, had added baggage into the suitcase called "Body Baggage." The baggage we carry in regard to our bodies can stem from multiple things: how others perceive it and treat us, how we perceive it and treat ourselves, name-calling and body shaming, as I had experienced from others and myself, and also these instances early on in life where we experience our body more sexually or romantically. It shapes our experiences in ways I never really thought of until I was vividly put back into this experience one day during therapy. Out of ALL the other countless crazier instances, the younger Dani showed up to bring this memory to the forefront, screaming about how she was still there and needed to resolve this. We must resolve the baggage because if we don't, it doesn't matter if you lose weight or get a nose job, a breast augmentation, or a **BBL**; that baggage will still be circling the carousel, waiting for you to pick it up. If you don't fix the thoughts in your brain, you can lose weight but will still think the same thoughts inside a smaller body. Those thoughts and beliefs don't simply disappear when your body changes, it follows you around; it's like taking everything out of your big suitcase and shoving it into a carry-on. It's all still there, just waiting to bust at the seams. Without fixing the tune between your two ears (thank you, Emily, for this saying), you'll always keep finding parts of your body you want to change or hide. Once you do the work to change your thoughts, you lose the extra baggage and feel lighter.

Maybe it's not your boobs for you, but another part of your body that you wish were smaller or bigger; I would bet there is something. One of my good friends has had a lot of attention because she has, in most people's opinion, a great ass. I never could understand why she made comments or felt self-conscious because of her hips or butt because there are so many people that literally have surgeries to have her figure. Much like me and having issues with clothing where buttons are about to pop open, or the seaming that should be under my boobs is now at the top of my chest, she also struggled with finding pants that would fit her hips and butt that didn't leave a gap at her back because of her slim waist. Or getting stared at a little too long when wearing a curve-fitting outfit; she gets a lot of unwanted attention, and even though her figure is so beautiful, she has brought some of that along with her in the present day.

At the end of the day, we deserve to feel comfortable and at home in our bodies, baggage-free. Whether you wish your body was curvier, slimmer, taller, or shorter; or less wrinkles or no cellulite; or you've had issues feeling comfortable saying no, or desperately trying to be invisible, you are carrying around body baggage. The trick is, the more we love our bodies for all their imperfections, the more we treat them with love and drop the shame, and the more that baggage slowly begins to fade away.

The million dollar question then is: "How do we learn to love our body?"

1.   *Work on your mirror talk.*

This is going to feel weird AF, I know. But while looking in the mirror, choose a part of your body you dislike the most. You know, the part that you put down, criticize, try to hide, THAT body part. Talk to it. Acknowledge the body part, and apologize for how you've treated it and spoken to it in the past. Now, say something positive, anything. I told you it's going to feel weird, just trust me, okay? Look, I'll give you an example. For a long time, I've really loathed my thighs. They are large, and despite any weight I've ever lost, they never seem to change size. I'm decently tall but have a long torso and short legs, so they feel stumpy. They rub together, I get chub rub, and they have lots of cellulite. I didn't wear shorts for years because of how much I hated my thighs. But… here is how I talk to them now. I gently touch my thighs and apologize for hiding, for criticizing and trying to shrink them into submission, for treating them like they weren't worthy because of their size. I acknowledge their strength. I feel the muscles in my quadriceps and show gratitude for keeping me standing daily. For the gift of being able to walk, swim, dance, and simply be. I tell them how much I love them for all they do and have done for me. And I repeat this as much as I need to. I know its weird, but if you can't show your body love and gratitude, you're always going to have the body baggage. I'm not suggesting you do this live on IG, but just try one positive word and one positive sentence in private. You deserve it.

2. Get comfortable being naked.

Yeah, I said it. How do you expect to release body baggage if you can't be naked in your own skin when no one is around but you? If you're avoiding the mirror every time you get out of the shower or keep the lights off so you or your partner can't see your body, you may feel at ease, but that baggage is there, my friend. Take a few minutes a day, a week, a month, to be naked. It gets easier, I promise. Sometimes, I do my makeup naked, and there is no way of hiding standing in front of the mirror this way. The more you do this, the more you realize after a minute or two that it's just a body, nothing more. This is the beauty of getting comfortable being naked. It releases the shame, expectations, and negativity and becomes a body in the mirror because that is ALL IT IS. We have made it so much more than that. So, strip it down for yourself, and get cozy in your birthday suit!

3. Positive body affirmations.

It may be woo-woo, and I may have already suggested affirmations, but I'm truly that passionate about how effective they can be on your journey to loving your body. It feels weird at first, but practicing a few positive affirmations specific to your body makes it feel more natural. Over time, you actually believe it. " My body is beautiful and strong." " I love my body for its amazingness." "I am grateful for my body for caring for me every day." These are a few of my favorites. Head out to google for additional affirmation options, test a few out, and repeat them, friend.

4. *Release the past, release comparison, and simply be present in your body.*

When we are constantly on the hamster wheel of trying to get back to "pre-pregnancy" weight, or a certain pant size, a number on the scale or comparing ourselves to anybody and everyone, we are not present in our body. We're disconnected and distracted. Instead of focusing on the past, ruminating in comparison, or making plans to lose weight, stay in the present. Breathe into your body. Feel where in your body you feel those fears and anxieties and give those spaces extra love. Being in the present moment ensures we are connected. This is a beautiful way to love and honor our bodies; besides, when has comparison ever helped you before?

5. *Treat your body like you give a shit.*

If you fill your body with garbage, never sleep, and sit on the couch all day in the dark, it's not surprising to anyone when you feel miserable, lethargic, and depressed. I'm not saying to become vegan, keto, or go crazy on food intake, no, ma'am. I'm saying to focus on fueling your body with nutritious foods, mostly from "real sources," not made in a lab. Drink lots of water. Enjoy indulgences with friends and family, sharing the experience in community and in deliciousness. Move your body—any way that doesn't feel like torture, just move it. We weren't destined to sit all day, and I promise you will feel good mentally doing so. SLEEP. You can't feel good when you don't sleep. So if you have to work on winding down earlier, shut off your phone, take a bath, light candles, recite a spell to the sleep gods, do it. Prioritizing sleep is a game changer. All these things will make your body feel lighter, and I swear you'll feel better all over. Doing these things because you GET TO and not because you HAVE TO will also change your relationship with your body. If you want to let go of the body baggage, treat your body like you give a shit. Baby steps, my love.

Chapter 3
Diet Demise

Raise your hand if you've ever been on a diet. Ok, I can't see you, but I imagine your hand is raised. I also imagine that if we were standing in a football stadium and I asked this question, most hands would be up in the sky. Hell, I would bet a million dollars that I'm right. Now, raise your other hand if you've been on multiple diets. I'd probably take the odds of double or nothing that most of you still had both hands in the air. That is how confident I am in the fact that most people have been on so many diets. Our entire society is diet-obsessed and values thinness above all. Well, I'm here to say, FUCK THAT!

By the time I was 11, I started my first diet. I am quite certain that between nine and eleven, I began trying to eat less intentionally. However, I distinctly remember the summer my best friend

Kristen's mom and mine were doing Weight Watchers. This was pre-digital Weight Watchers, and calculating points was done a'la sliding scale on laminated paper, and we thought we would follow suit. We had zero idea what the hell we were doing, but we started memorizing certain food points and trying to make our own little point calculators. When that became way too complicated, we started following a low-carb diet. This was back when Atkins came out, and it was all the rage. My mom and Kristen's dad had both started this diet and had successfully lost a substantial amount of weight. So we gave it a try too. Friday night pizza nights, and there we were at 11 years old, eating just the fucking pizza toppings and leaving the crust on our plates. Kristen's dad was not impressed and made her stop. I'm not sure if my mom caught what I was doing or just let it slide, but it didn't last very long because no carbs at 11 years old is brutal—who am I kidding—no carbs at any age is brutal!

The summer before junior high, I remember waking up early to swim laps on an empty stomach and seeing how long I could go without eating. When I did eat, it was always low-calorie, low-fat, low-quality garbage. I would order a salad or some low-calorie--will be hungry again in an hour--bullshit meal if I went out with friends. If they asked why I wasn't partaking in nachos, potato skins, burgers, and fries, I would simply say I was training for sports. I don't know if anyone actually believed me, but no one said anything otherwise.

For a long time, I was so disconnected from my body, never paying attention to what it needed, what it wanted, or what it felt. In high school, I teeter tottered between both wanting attention from the opposite sex and also wanting to be hidden in the shadows, away from anyone's glances. This spiraled out of control after my grandmother—my mammaw died. My emotions were so stuck. I was broken and, yet, never asked for help. Always told people I was fine, knowing deep down I was hurting badly. I lost interest in things that used to bring me joy—playing sports and joining clubs and activities. I withdrew. I would starve myself all day, or maybe I'd have 2 clementines at lunch, careful not to eat much in front of others. I never wanted people to look at me and think, "No wonder she's so fat; look at how she eats." In private, however, behind closed doors, or in my car, I would binge.

I wish I could have seen it then. I was so sad that the only thing I felt I could control and could comfort me was food. I remember going to Taco Bell after school, being careful to hide the wrappers under other trash in the trash can, or eating in my car, and throwing away any evidence at the gas station. If I didn't stop for fast food after starving myself all day, I would stop at the gas station and buy a soda, bag of chips, and some kind of candy or Little Debbie cake. This was my drug, my sweet release, and my dirty little secret. Inevitably, I started gaining weight. I think subconsciously, this was also my way of hiding from unwanted attention. I know it seems so counterintuitive, but for some reason and on some level, I felt more comfortable with being barely glanced at and cast away as the fat girl than to be ogled at and have comments made on my boobs or any other part of my body.

Here's the thing, though, as my dirty secret continued, it got harder to control. It was controlling me. I was so embarrassed and felt so much shame. Honestly, this is the first time I'm actually acknowledging this behavior out loud. I always felt my body was the problem. I have carried that unworthiness about my body for far longer than I ever would want to admit, and sadly, I know that I'm not alone. In some ways, I think things are both harder and easier nowadays. When I was a teenager, social media didn't exist yet, so I didn't have a non-stop comparison loop on my phone (thank God). We also didn't have popular curvy women in media or any kind of inclusivity messaging on sizes. Most stores now have all sizes in the women's department housed together, but growing up, you had regular up to size 14, maybe 16 if you were lucky, and then it was a separate plus size section, often on the other side of the store or on a different floor. Why the fuck do we do that? Clothes are needed for all bodies; why do we need to segregate it to make people feel shitty? Also, the plus-size clothing options were terrible until Torrid came around. You would have to go to a department store plus size section, and good luck finding anything that didn't look like a goddamned moomoo. The shame I used to feel having to go to specialty stores for my clothes and having to pay so much more for trendy plus-size clothes was palpable.

My aunt and I used to go shopping every year before my birthday or Christmas to look for new clothes or shoes. I always looked forward to those times with her until I had to start shopping in the plus size section. From that point on, I would aggressively try to lose weight before our shopping trip, only to fail and spend time admiring clothes that would never fit my fat body. The feeling of unworthiness because my body continued to grow, and my time spent on diets grew as it did. It took me **YEARS** to realize that diets don't fucking work, so let's get into why.

Let's test a theory, shall we? For the rest of this chapter, don't think about puppies. Not about how cute they are or when they have the zoomies, or when their tails wag so fast that their whole butt shakes, or how they are so stinking adorable it brings a smile to your face. You're thinking of puppies, aren't you? Even though I said not to. You weren't thinking of dogs, but now your brain is inundated with thoughts of pups, huh? Same. And this is one of the reasons why diets don't work. Before you come at me, when I say diet, I mean a restrictive diet; I don't mean a way of eating. Those are vastly different things, ok. Psychologically, when we decide to cut something out of our lives, that is all we think about. For the same reason, you're thinking of puppies or when you decide to kick the toxic man out of your life. You keep thinking of what he is doing, trying to resist texting him or checking his social media, or as soon as you decide to break up with desserts, all you seem to think about is ice cream, brownies, and any hit of sugar; you're telling yourself you can't think of those things and that's now the brain's prime focus. When we start a diet, our brain obsesses over the feeling of lack. All we're thinking about is all the things we CAN'T have, and we're not even enjoying any of the things we actually can have. So when we cut out desserts, suddenly you have a full set of sweet teeth, drooling over anything that will give you that sugar fix. Come on, it is not feasible to believe you will never have dessert again in your life. So when we follow restrictive diets, we essentially white knuckle it until we are done with the diet, and then inevitably, we enjoy those indulgences again and in excess because we've been deprived for so long that we gain weight. Then we think we need to have more control, so we go back to the restrictive diet, lose weight, and the cycle continues on a never-ending loop.

Have you ever done a low-carb diet? BITCH, it is awful. (Side note, when I say bitch, it's really a term of endearment, we're friends now, right?) Low carbs will cause you to drop pounds faster than Ozempic. I remember thinking the first time I did this diet, it wasn't so bad, but let me tell you, my low-carb diet was SO unhealthy. My arteries are still probably semi-clogged because of it. Fast food double cheeseburgers without the bun, pizza toppings, bacon, sausage, pepperoni, deli meat, ALL THE CHEESE. But as soon as I started this diet, I craved any carb you could imagine; I'm talking, I would dream of sandwich bread—the garbage white bland shit that tastes terrible, I didn't care, give me BREAD! Bread isn't even something I want most of the time unless it's worth it, and most breads, unless they are bakery-made or fresh, are simply not. So what the hell was I doing "cheating" by sneaking into the kitchen at night eating sandwich bread, hot dog buns, or any kind of bread-adjacent item I could get my hands on when I didn't really like any of it? Diets, they really make sense huh? Also, doesn't it seem wild that a diet could literally suggest you cut out entire food groups? Don't eat fruit or any kind of vegetable with a higher carb count. Villainizing rice because it has so many carbs and god forbid, you eat a potato! Excuse me, what?

You know what else I hate about "diets"? If you're creative, and let's be honest, if you're on a diet, you're creative with food, girl, you can make unhealthy garbage fit your diet. Yes, I have extra points, so I'm going to eat a bunch of " free " vegetables so I can eat french fries, drink half a bottle of wine, or eat fast food. Back in my early 20s, that is exactly what I did. I was following Weight Watchers and used to stop for a bagel and coffee on the way to work, Chipotle or Subway for lunch, some kind of BS frozen dinner, and a fiber one brownie or low-fat bland vanilla ice cream for dinner. What actual nutrients did I even consume? Hint—not many. This is what I mean: following a diet does not mean nutritious, filling, good-quality food.

It simply means finding ways to work creatively within the system. I don't know about you, but the older I get, the more I am interested in quality, delicious and nutritious foods.

While we're on the topic, let me tell you about doing keto and trying to hit a 70% fat macro target each day. It doesn't seem like it would be that difficult, but it is when you're also eating protein. I would eat what I thought was a perfect keto diet all day and still not be at a 70% fat macro. So what would I do? Make decaf coffee with MCT oil and butter at night after dinner to ensure I get up to 70%. I'll tell you, I felt pretty good on keto, but it was so unsustainable, and also— eating butter and MCT oil simply to hit a macro seemed so fucking dumb.

I KNOW I'm not the only one with this kind of story. Let me ask you, how did you feel after being on a diet? Empowered? Balanced? Man, I hope you did, but I can tell you that diets only compounded my obsessive thoughts about food and ultimately made me feel like shit about myself. All I did was think about food. What I could eat, what I couldn't eat, and what I was going to eat. If I were going to a restaurant with friends, I'd check the menu beforehand to get an idea of what would be "approved," all for the sake of remaining "on plan". It was fucking exhausting, and honestly, it is NOT normal to think about food all day long. Inevitably, after "failing" at whatever diet I was following, I would always end up thinking that I was the problem, I lacked willpower, I lacked motivation, and was constantly left deflated and disappointed in myself. I never once questioned if it was the diet's fault.

THIS IS DIET CULTURE!

Diet culture wants you to feel this way. It wants to kick you while you are down. Rub it in your face that someone else dropped weight and succeeded while you're sitting on the couch shoveling ice cream in your mouth and rolling your eyes, thinking, "So good for you, Jill, you lost weight; here's your fucking trophy." It quite literally makes a shit ton of money off your demise, off making you feel like a worthless piece of shit because diet culture knows that when you're at your lowest, all it takes is a social media post, or an ad, or something to show the new weight loss craze and it will have you right back where it wants you; buying whatever they are selling.

Here is the thing: food is delicious! Food brings people together; it's the cornerstone of gatherings. As humans, we are biologically wired to crave community. If I have to go to one more gathering where someone compliments the amazingly delicious food and then in the next breath makes a disparaging comment on their body, or how this isn't on their diet, or anything of the sort, I may lose it, you've been warned. One piece of incredible lasagna, cake, glass of wine, or whatever, is not what caused you to gain weight and will not make you obese from one serving. Suppose we're breaking bread (delicious, worth-it bread) and enjoying killer company. In that case, we are NOT talking calories or anything of the sort.

I had this epiphany one day and asked myself, "Am I going to be on a diet for the rest of my fucking life?" I shuddered at the thought. I had already spent WAY too much time and energy being trapped in this yo-yo life of diet, restrict, binge, repeat, and I couldn't think of spending any more time being trapped. I realized that diet culture is a profiteer of insecurities. They always have some new product to sell, and shocker, it's not meant to make us actually feel our best selves. It's intended to keep us in the diet loop and ensure we're a long-term customer, honey!

If you're tired of living on the hamster wheel—and I hope you are—here are my top tips for leaving diet culture to the wayside.

1. Delete your calorie-counting apps and food trackers and hide your scale.

Relax, relax; I'm not saying you can't return to these ever, but maybe take a slight break. You've likely been living in a world where you weigh yourself daily—and I'd guess your mood is determined by the outcome—is that really serving you? Maybe your experience is different than mine, but inputting every piece of food into a tracker did nothing but make me obsessed with food. Planning, tracking, thinking about what I would eat next, when will I eat, can I eat this, should I eat that, how many calories does this have, how many carbs are in this, how much protein? This is not a way to live long-term. Like most things, we can use an audit—maybe monthly, maybe quarterly, you choose. See if you've mostly maintained your weight, are you getting adequate nutrition, do you feel your best? I think an audit is reasonable, but otherwise, are we living the rest of our lives tracking our calories and macros? Please, God, no.

2. If a diet suggests cutting out whole food groups—actual nutrient food groups - maybe don't follow?

I am not a medical doctor, nutritionist, dietitian, or anything related. However, I have read countless nutrition books and done my own studies. There are certain conditions where it is necessary to cut back on starchy carbs or reduce overall carbohydrate intake. But I don't believe eliminating all carbohydrates is best for the majority. I am of the personal opinion for long-term success that, if a diet tells you to eliminate fruit, or perhaps any kind of starchy vegetable, potatoes, or corn… it's just not going to be sustainable. Again—this gets into the obsessive nature of dieting, and it's not a way to live. There are extremes to everything, I get it. So if you're eating bowls of fruit all day, every day, ok, that's likely a lot of sugar, and I'd imagine you don't feel your best. But also, if you're going to eat bowls of something every day, it could be a hell of a lot worse than fruit. This is just my big sister's advice, especially if you're a woman. Food group elimination is a challenging route to take, and I think it should be an indication not to do it.

3. Pay attention to how you feel and not how you look.

Say what you want, but you can "look" great and feel miserable. You can look "heavy" and feel amazing. You can be losing weight and feel terrible. You can be following a diet perfectly and have zero energy, have major gas, and overall feel like shit. This is why I think paying attention to how foods make you feel is the most important thing. We all are slightly different. Some people can eat pancakes for breakfast and pasta for dinner and feel fine. Me? Get my bed ready because I'm going to be in the fetal position with a belly that looks 8 months pregnant, and praying for my end. For some people, living a vegetarian or vegan lifestyle feels great, but for others, it does not. At the end of the day, isn't it more about how you feel? Your energy levels and not being bloated AF as opposed to your dress size? Use how you feel as your guidepost. I truly believe you will be happier overall and have a better relationship with food.

4. Everything in moderation, not restriction.

I know moderation is an annoying word; believe me. Somedays, I want to eat the whole bag of chips, ya know? But my point is that instead of completely eliminating something you genuinely love, how about trying moderation? Just like my puppy example from earlier, if you tell yourself you will never again eat chips, you won't be happy when you meet friends out for Mexican. In fact, you'll be thinking about that deliciousness so much you probably won't even be present to your awesome company. One strategy I like to implement is, lets say I really want chips or a brownie, how can I make this meal more balanced so that I can not only have the chips and brownies but also have foods that will give me nutrients and leave me full? For me, that looks like maybe getting a salad and some chips. Or chips with some hummus and veggies. That way, I'm pairing natural nutrients to give my body what it needs and what I want. You'll almost always see me eat a salad with pizza for this exact reason. This makes it feel like a win/win situation, and I'm here for that.

5. *You're more than you're damn weight or looks.*

I think I get so absolutely pissed now about this because we are so much more than our bodies and appearance. Yet, more people than not obsess about what they look like and how much they weigh, constantly trying to make themselves smaller and look younger. We have so much more to offer than our physical appearance, and as soon as we realize this, love this, and are confident in this, the life-changing magic begins. Whenever I want to comment about my appearance or experience my friend doing the same, I send love and move on. We're human, but damnit, women are so amazing. We have to stop being so small. We're incredible—let your light shine, girl. We need it more than we need you to be a size 4, ok?

Chapter 4
Dating, patterns, and the patriarchy

If you were one of the lucky ones to have met the love of your life in high school or during college and never had the *pleasure* of online dating or dating in the 2020s, consider yourself lucky. In this chapter, I want to talk about how your past shows up in your current dating life and how your past can affect patterns in any kind of relationship. And, of course, we couldn't talk about men without noting the patriarchy and how women are treated, not only in relationships but in the workplace and elsewhere.

By now, we've already spent what feels like a lifetime discussing my chronic issues with my body, lack of confidence, and overall low self-esteem, so I'm going to do my best not to be redundant, but it should be no surprise to anyone that all of those issues affect dating, how we're perceived by our peers in the workplace, and generally in all instances. These issues aren't isolated to one aspect of life, rather, they permeate into all the cracks and crevices, hence why it's so important to fix your shit. The fact of the matter is that despite ALL the work, sometimes the past doesn't always stay in the past; it's buried deep.

In college, I studied business and Spanish, so naturally, I wanted to find a part-time job where I could practice my language skills or at least be surrounded by it. I ended up working part-time at a local, family-owned Colombian restaurant. I definitely got my wish to be surrounded by the Spanish language and have opportunities to practice. The other skills I didn't know I needed or wanted to learn were talking to strangers, honing my sales skills, and working with difficult people and working in challenging environments. I was a good server; despite my insecurities, dealing with people came naturally to me, and it always has, for the most part. In fact, it was those four years spent working in that restaurant, chatting it up with strangers and even having "regulars," that made me think I could be decent in sales.

I dabbled in a few different job paths after leaving the restaurant. In my first "real" job when I was 23, I told a coworker how I wanted to work in sales, and I distinctly remember her telling me I wasn't assertive enough. Ah, if only you knew me now :). I leaped into a financial advisor training program with the idea that this was my dream job; I had the people skills and a degree in finance, and this would be a path destined to offer me wealth. Needless to say, I got knocked down quite a few pegs. I passed what they said was the hardest exam, the Series 7, where at that time, you had one shot at passing or adios to your job, only to fail the Series 66 (the regulatory exam) twice, hence losing my job anyways. My self-confidence was crushed. Believing this was my destined career path, I began working at another firm that didn't require as many licenses. I can genuinely say that a career as a financial advisor or life insurance agent is NOT my dream job—targeting my family and friends as prospects was my nightmare. Without a job and a clue what kind of career path I wanted to pursue, I naturally jumped back into the restaurant industry. It felt like I was wasting away with shame at my tumble down the ladder from a potential financial advisor at Morgan Stanley with an MBA, to now a restaurant manager (not that I think anything is wrong with this whatsoever, but at this age, my ego was embarrassed and pissed to be paying student loans with nothing to show for it.) One lucky day, a former coworker contacted me to discuss an outside sales opportunity. He was being promoted to sales manager and needed to hire his replacement, and he thought of me. I desperately wanted to break into the sales world. I knew this would be a great step; even better, it would get me out of that period of self-loathing.

I felt confident with my interviews and was hopeful I'd have a job offer. Ultimately, I did, but it was not without my friend and former coworker telling me that the Vice President did not want to hire me. Woof. I could have gone without knowing that part, but my friend was a wide-open book and always told the WHOLE, at times, unnecessary story. I would go on to work at that company for nearly seven years, and I NEVER forgot that the vice president, the second in command of the company, did not want to hire me. A huge part of me thought it was because of my appearance.

When I started at this company, I was the largest I had ever been in my life. I was deeply depressed on the inside but didn't show it; I don't even think I realized it at the time. On my starting day, I was accompanied by a woman who became my friend but looked like a real-life Barbie doll. Beautiful, blonde, thin, sweet, and genuinely caring. What a stark contrast we made. She was the center of attention, and I felt like the ugly stepsister. Furthermore, her sales territory was arguably the best—closest to the office, worked the most in the past, less driving, and more brand awareness. Mine was one of the least worked and farthest drives (I was really bitter and negative, clearly). Despite all this, I was determined to make this career work and take advantage of this opportunity. In the midst of my first full year at this company, I was dumped—by that same guy

I talked about earlier- and I went on a downward spiral. I was drinking too much, going out on random tinder dates—seeking external validation in any way I possibly could. I was a hot mess.

After all that bullshit, I started taking better care of myself, and I slowly lost some weight. Actually, I lost about 70 pounds in total. I started straightening my hair instead of letting the natural curls show and jazzed up my wardrobe. Let me tell you, my sales soared even more, and the attention I received at the company also increased. So much for letting your work show for you, huh? I should be easier on people; my self-confidence had increased, and I think that also had a lot to do with it, not that fat shaming isn't a thing. I was not used to the attention, and I still felt like that girl who was 70lbs heavier. Nonetheless, I started relying on my looks more and more. I constantly had to have FULL makeup done, hair straightened, rocking heels, the works, every single day. Being in sales, which is male-dominated, can be annoying at times, but I grew to really enjoy working with men. No BS, you knew where you stood, and there was no drama. I was down with that. Working with men, though, there were times, especially when happy hours were involved, that the professional lines could get a little blurred.

Sales could often feel almost like flirting was the way to get more sales; in fact, my boss often joked about how he would do just that with women to get an in. The number of meetings I have been in where I've felt a man run his eyes up and down my body is countless. I've had prospects text me on my personal cell phone, follow me on social media, and ask me out via email. I've dealt with it all while keeping a smile on my face despite my insides being in knots. Since my income depended on sales, I often dealt with it. What else could I do? There was this one instance that was more egregious than others. I had been working to obtain a new account. It was a really large account, and I had spent countless hours, visits, and proposal revisions with this company trying to make the sale. My boss (who was only a few years older than me) and I stopped by the potential client to see if we could get an update on their decision. As we're standing in the lobby talking with the IT Manager (male), he starts mentioning their incumbent vendor, how the sales rep was trying to do all she could to keep the account, and how she was really good. He then says, "But if we compare her and Dani, especially in looks, Dani wins." He nudges and winks at my boss while looking me up and down. The patriarchy is so fun. I just stood there and cracked a smile; what the fuck else could I do?

Another instance was on a sales incentive trip where my friend (the one who looked like Barbie) and I were the only female sales reps who had qualified. When we arrived at dinner, the VP of Sales tells us, "I know why we are so successful; it's because of the beautiful sales reps we have." This was at least a nice comment, but all it did was reinforce that my looks were everything. My worth, income, and being all depended on how I looked.

I'm ashamed to admit that I relished the attention—inappropriate or not-- for a few years. I had not done all the healing work, and I was seeking approval outside of myself and valuing men's approval of me, whether they were coworkers, superiors, in a relationship, single, or even married. It was not a good look, and I'll say there are still times I look back and have to forgive myself for regretful decisions. The point is that we take the hurt from our past into our future. We seek to fill the void in whatever way we can. I tried to fill the void of feeling unworthy and not loving myself by seeking validation from men. But the past doesn't vanish if you don't deal with it. I never addressed my lack of self-confidence, feelings of unworthiness, or the dislike for my body. This is exactly why they say you can lose weight, but you have to fix the inside, or else you'll still face those internal demons, just from within a smaller body.

Let's go back to when I was starting to date, post-breakup, with that guy who's gotten more press than I would like (damnit). I was seeking validation. I was seeking any evidence to prove that inner Barb voice was wrong, that my ex was not in fact the only man who would ever desire me and that there were plenty of men interested in me. Turns out Barb was so wrong. There were a ton of men interested in me, though a high majority were only interested in me physically.   The first guy I went out with after the big breakup was such a fuck boy, but I was oblivious; I had been out of the game, and this was my first rodeo on Tinder (which, by the way, had only been around for like a year at this point in time). Let's call him Jack. Jack only wanted to hang out at night and only at my place, (I actually think he may have still been living with his mom). There were no dates outside of the first meet-up where he proceeded to shove his tongue down my throat after walking me to my car outside of a fucking Applebees. Our texts were exclusively flirtatious and often sexual in nature. Despite recognizing this behavior as inappropriate, I found myself starved for attention and allowed it to continue, assuming it was the new normal. Then, one night, I was out with a friend and spotted him with another girl; WOOF! I was crushed. The combination of that experience, plus the previously unfaithful boyfriend and an overall lifetime struggle of vulnerability, well, I started building walls around myself, brick by brick, and then covered them in fucking ice. Herein, some really horrible dating patterns began, and (sigh) I'm still working through things in this area today.

As a 'fuck you' to the patriarchy, and for the sake of locking up my heart, I took a page out of the male playbook. I would get someone interested and never let them in fully. I would never even give them a chance; instead, I was just there to hook up and keep it moving. I went through a phase where I was moving through life with nothing but masculine energy, and it was fun, but it was also lonely AF at times. I would go through these phases of taking breaks from dating and then jump back in just to fall into the same patterns.

I'd end up being attracted to emotionally unavailable men (or committed men), all because it protected me from truly putting myself out there. I would find the smallest reason to get the ick; he's shorter than me, works at a grocery store, is a picky eater (all real-life reasons), and I'd be done. No second chance; have a wonderful life. Not something to be proud of, but I was the cut-off queen; one strike and you're out. After several rounds of this nonsense, I'd end up exhausted, fed up, vowing that all men suck and I'd be single for the rest of my life.

Recently, I relocated to another state and decided to give dating another chance. Let me tell you, those habits run deep and are difficult to break! Now, however, I've become more self-aware and put a lot of effort into self-improvement. At least now, I can recognize my own shortcomings sometimes. Have you ever heard of attachment theory? I stumbled upon it just as I was reentering the dating scene, and I've never felt so understood. The attachment style theory stems from your childhood and how you were shown love and felt security from your primary caregiver. This can cause you to develop a certain type of attachment that can affect your relationships. While I think I'm a bit of a mix, I have to realize that, in some instances, I'm quite avoidant. It explains why I have struggled with vulnerability in trusting others to accept my feelings, why I rely mostly on myself, and why I'm pretty quick to cut men out. Again, it's a defense mechanism to protect myself from getting hurt. As I started dating more and having multiple dates with the same person, I realized I could be either very avoidant or very anxious. I think the anxiousness stems from having a prior partner who was unfaithful to me. I'm still not a master at dating, but in the last year, I'm getting a little better; but damn, do I still tend to get hung up on men who I KNOW aren't it, or get exhausted by men's nonsensical behavior. The thing is, the more we deal with the past, the more we heal the past, and the better our futures can be. I hate to tell you, but if you sweep every emotion and trauma under the rug, it's going to come up at some point and almost always in the most inopportune time (more on this later). Most importantly, though, patterns develop, and once we notice them and can reflect, we can assess and change direction. The patriarchy, well, we are all making strides in the right direction, but let's face it, it's going to be a while before it's completely dismantled, so focus on what we can control and vigilantly stand up for yourself.

My top tips on dating, patterns, and the MF patriarchy:

1. *Seek internal validation above all else.*

Being desired, wanted, and complimented feels great. I will never argue that. Tell me I'm pretty, beautiful, gorgeous, and sexy all day. But if I can't see that in myself, if I don't know those words to be true, then they're not meaningful. It doesn't matter if someone else thinks you're amazing and beautiful if you don't. Until you spend time with yourself, are comfortable alone, and know your worth has nothing to do with what someone else feels about you, it's going to be challenging. You likely will continue seeking outside validation to fill in the hole you aren't filling up for yourself. We all are human, and some days are harder than others. Some days, I feel like the biggest loser on the planet and think there is something wrong with me because I'm still single, but I know none of this to be true. If I wanted to fill every night with a different man, I could. If I wanted someone to keep me company and keep my bed warm, it would be easy. But doing that simply not to be alone makes me feel even more lonely. It's a quick dopamine hit like a band-aid patching up a geyser overflowing with water. It will never be enough. The quickest path forward is to develop a relationship with yourself and treat yourself how you would want someone to treat you. Date yourself. Know your worth, and never settle for anything less than you deserve.

## 2.	*Choose your battles wisely.*

I may get some hate for this statement, but here is the thing I believe: if we spend every waking moment fighting the patriarchy, we're going to be consumed and have nothing left to give. This is why I say pick your battles wisely. I say that also because this becomes easier once you work on mastering tip number one. Suppose you're not seeking validation from men. In that case, you're less likely to deal with their shit and the uneven balance that is a result of the patriarchy. Now, some men need to be called out. When I meet a man and start chatting, and before we've met, he starts sending unsolicited pictures, asking me for pictures, and being overly sexual. I call those boys out. I'm not dealing with it, and in my opinion, the women who do are the women who need to work on tip number one the most. If I've never met you, you're not my boyfriend, or we haven't cultivated that type of relationship, you're not to be sexting me, period. You haven't earned that right yet, my guy. Also, overly commenting on my body pre-meeting, you're going to be told how I am much more than my body because I AM. I recently had a man who told me "oh, you are so gorgeous and thicker than cold peanut butter." This was after he would send about 5 selfies a day that I NEVER asked for and before I ever had met him in person. I politely said, "ok, I think we need to pause because I can appreciate your taste and preferences, but I am so much more than my body, and I'm not here for this kind of conversation when we have never met in person." But if I called out every man who stared at me too long, was a creep, or the sales bullshit I've had to deal with, I would never get anything else done. So, hence, my idea of picking your battles.

3. *Analyze patterns and determine their root cause.*

If you keep finding yourself dating the same kind of losers and wondering what gives, I think it's time you start to reflect on your patterns. This is where I realized I am attracted to unavailable men because it's a way to protect myself. I also struggle with vulnerability and relying on others because not only was I cheated on and then left, but losing my dad slowly over the 10 years of his battling Alzheimer's weighed heavily on me. It made me feel like I had to rely on myself because men in my life always left. I know that doesn't sound fair; it wasn't my dad's choice, but that's how it feels sometimes. His sickness scarred me a lot. I've been to therapy and continue to work on this, but it made me feel like no one could understand me, and I didn't feel safe opening up to people about my struggles. I stopped trying to date seriously for years because I didn't know how to let people into that situation. I felt like I had to be strong for my mom; my brother dealt with his emotions even less than me, and I didn't think any of my friends could understand, so how could some new dude get it? This is why I started being interested in unavailable men; it kept me at arm's length, which was easier. If we never connect the dots, we are doomed to continue these patterns that are hardwired into our brains! If you want to change, if you want to attract a better partner, and stop allowing losers access to you, deal with your fucking patterns and where they come from. It's not going to be instant rainbows and sunshine afterward, but slowly, it will become easier to understand and to give yourself love. You'll know it's not you that is the problem, and that is huge growth.

Chapter 5
Comparison and Societal Bullshit

The "expected" path of progression, as dictated by society, is complete and utter bullshit. It sets unattainable expectations, and if you don't meet them, it leaves you feeling like a complete piece of shit and a failure. Let's unpack this, ok?

When you were growing up, assuming you are a female, what was your life plan expected to be? Did it go a little something like get good grades in school so you can get into a good college, do well in college so you can land a good job, and in between that time, find a man, get married, have kids, buy a home and live happily ever after? That's what I expected, what I thought would just magically unfold in front of me at exactly the perfect time. Spoiler alert, shit did not go down that way for me. So what happens when you skip a step of this path? People look at you weirdly, like you're contagious or a fucking side-show freak. Let's not even start with if you do follow the "right" path and are still left feeling completely miserable. How can you possibly complain? It's bullshit.

Let's start this chapter with when we follow the path, yeah? Growing up, my family valued education, and good grades were definitely expected. I took to most things naturally, not to sound conceited, but I didn't really study until I got to college. In fact, I rarely took homework home and carried around a book to read "for fun" because I would inevitably be done with my work and have nothing to do. Obviously, I was not challenged much in high school. College, I had a rude awakening because I had zero idea how to study, and now I was surrounded by students who had already taken classes that my high school didn't offer. I struggled. What was even harder than trying to figure out how to study was deciding what the hell I wanted to do with the rest of my life and the dreaded task of picking a major. Honestly, why are we expected to know this answer at 18 or 19 years old? I knew I wanted to have a career involving international business, other cultures, and languages; I wanted to study Spanish but didn't want to be a teacher. I remember my favorite junior high school teacher, my first experience with learning Spanish, and also the tour guide for my first trip to Europe—where

I knew I was destined to travel and learn other languages and cultures—telling me how she had to find other avenues to keep her skills sharp, otherwise, with teaching Spanish 1, you could easily lose a lot of that knowledge. Besides, I didn't want to teach students who were only taking the classes out of obligation, no thanks. I would have wanted to teach students like me who were passionate about learning another language and culture so that at least I could scratch teaching from the list of possible career paths.

For the first two years at my VERY expensive liberal arts university, I took mostly required courses. It wasn't until my junior year that I truly got into classes for my major. Half of my time at college was spent taking classes that had little to do with my actual major. What happens when you realize in year three that you hate your chosen major? Yep, you guessed it; more time and more money spent trying to figure things out. I decided to major in International Business and Spanish, which I felt pretty good about until taking International Marketing, International Management, and International Economics in my junior year. I quickly realized that I needed something more specialized than simply International Business. It felt like I'd just end up being the jack of all trades, master of none business person, so I ended up declaring Finance as my major. Why? Well, it was the only core business class I halfway liked, and I assumed it would lead to a nice salary. Little did I know that I would be graduating with a degree in Finance and Spanish—after having been told that business degrees would provide a great career with a comfortable salary—in the midst of the financial crisis of 2008. Yep. So much for doing the "right thing." I found myself competing for entry-level jobs with people my parent's age because the economy was crashing. With my $100,000 education, I started my full-time server career. Cool. I slowly started to find my way, especially as the economy rebounded, but it took about a year for me to land a full-time gig (that had zero to do with my degree). By that time, it was time to start repaying my student loans, and I was earning a very entry-level salary. (I'm not going to get on my soapbox about how asinine the cost of education or health insurance is because I could probably write another book on both, but I will say that student loans are predatory.) Dani followed the perfect societal plan so far; good grades got the degree and then got fucked by the economy.

During this interesting time in my life of being a full-time server, I met a man—yes, that same over-publicized man- and we dated for 6 years, splitting up right before I turned 29. Right up to the day I found myself packing my shit and moving out, I thought I had checked off the "find a husband" box, negative. As my friend circle and his began marrying off, I assumed the proposal would be coming any day. We had been together for years, after all. While cleaning, I found evidence of something he had hidden to use in the proposal, which he confirmed later to me while also sharing that he had doubts about us and decided against it (in hindsight, I'm so thankful).

If I could tell you the amount of times people have asked me, "How can someone like you be single?" "How are you not married?" "You're so beautiful; how are you single?" You'd probably be shocked, and if I got money every time something to that effect was said to me, I probably could have paid for at least a year of college. Just a week ago, I had two instances within 12 hours. A colleague, in a sense, someone I have done business with, sent me a message congratulating me (we're Facebook friends) on having been in my new home for 6 months. He then proceeded to ask me if my family moved with me, no. "Did you and your husband split up?" *No, I'm single.* "I don't believe you." *Well, I am not married; I am single.* "There is no way someone as beautiful and amazing as you are is single." *Well, here I am.* "You were married, though?" *No,* . I mean, on and on this went, and he still never believed me. Maybe it's a cultural thing; I should probably move. I mean, my taxi driver in Mexico earlier this year had the same reaction. When I told him I was single, according to him, there was no way I'd be single if I lived in Mexico. The next morning, I was teaching a yoga class and had a new woman join. We talked after class, and she told me it was only her second class. She was trying to get back to it when I mentioned I had just moved to town 6 months ago, and she asked if I was married. Nope. "Oh my, you're so beautiful, though!" To which I said,

"Thank you. If you know anyone single, set me up!" I know the intentions of these statements are from a good place; they are compliments, albeit backhanded. But for me, it feels like another instance of what the fuck is wrong with me? (The answer? Nothing!) As someone who always thought her body size was the problem, all these situations on a bad day can make those old insecurities rise to the surface. Those days, I remind myself I'm the MF (motherfucking) prize. I will not settle for something less than I deserve; if I end up single for eternity, so be it. I love myself enough to know my worth, what I deserve, and what makes me happy. My life is good as it is, so unless someone can bring value to my life (and me to theirs), I'm staying single.

The evidence of how doing all the "right" things doesn't always go well is apparent. I'm not saying that it's not admirable to want this path; no, there is nothing wrong with wanting to start a career, find your partner, and have kids, but the pressure to do so is not ok. It's also the criticism you receive when your path is zigzagged instead of straight. I have friends, and I know you have married friends, where people constantly ask them, "So when are you going to have kids?" Honestly, why do people do this? It's none of their business; even if it's a close family member or friend, it's still not their business, and their pressure doesn't help. I've had close friends and family who don't want to have kids. I've also had close friends who want to have kids, but doing so hasn't been easy. These are all examples again as to why doing the right fucking thing doesn't always work and can leave you feeling like a failure. All these people found their partner, and they even got married, but whether they want to have kids and are silently struggling to conceive or don't want kids, they've now fallen into this weird societal limbo, which adds unnecessary pressure, unnecessary comparison, and unnecessary overthinking. Just like I get annoyed when people ask me why I'm still single, can you imagine what it must feel like when people ask when you're going to have kids while you're trying to do so? Maybe you're even going through IVF to become pregnant, and some bozo asks you, "Don't you want to have kids?" No, I just want to spend thousands and thousands of dollars to feel like a science experiment, be injected with hormones, pricked, prodded, and have my husband give me shots with needles half the size of my arms for the fun of it! And God forbid you don't want to have kids; you may as well light a bible on fire in front of people at the reaction. Are you starting to understand why societal pressures and expectations are complete bullshit?

Let's say you went through all the steps of this wonderfully "right" path. Then you wake up one day and feel nothing but misery. You look around, realizing you don't know your spouse anymore, you don't know who you are anymore, and it's evident you've been going through the motions all these years. You can't help but think that life is too short to feel so empty. Or what if you have a spouse, kids, career, and home, and then you realize you're spouse has been cheating on you? You did all the right things, so why do they all feel so fucking wrong?

As you can see, societal expectations force us into a game of comparison, sizing people up to see where they're at in the "right path" game and either feeling good about how we seemingly are doing better or feeling like shit that we're behind our peers. Comparison is worthless. I've known far too many people who, on the outside or on social media, appear to be the perfect family, perfect couple, or perfect person but are miserably unhappy. Herein lies the reason to stop comparing, stop competing, and just fucking be. You can be trashing yourself because you're not married, don't have as much money, or don't have a house or kids. Yet, that person you think has it **ALL** is actually putting on a show; meanwhile, they go to bed alone and miserable every night in their "perfect" world. Live your life, and don't worry how you stack up, friend.

Here are my top tips for getting past societal pressures and comparison:

1. *Blaze your own path if you need to.*

Blazing your own path can sometimes feel lonely, but it's necessary to undo the pressures and expectations that society and the world have bestowed upon us. So what if your life doesn't resemble a Hallmark Christmas movie (whose does?) So what if you haven't checked off all the boxes, or you're still figuring it all out? Do you! If you don't fit the mold, make your own mold. I read an article recently about how millennials are one of the first generations who are shifting the mold—not getting married, not having kids, or having a different lifestyle, like remote work, digital work, etc. and how it can feel lonely at times because there is no guidepost. It can feel "off" because we don't have anything to measure it by. I think that is fucking beautiful. We're forging a new direction and image for all who come after us. So blaze your own path, baby; we need all the representation we can get!

2. *Know the difference between the highlight reel and real life.*

 The longer the anniversary dedication on social media, the worse the relationship. Ok, I'm kidding, kind of. But really, it's easy to show up online as the perfect person and the perfect family, but how is that real? I surely don't wake up everyday shitting rainbows, do you? Some days suck, and I think we need to show the suck as much as we show the amazing days. Think about this when you fall into the trap of comparison. Does this person you're spiraling about only show the highlights wrapped in a beautiful bow? Does everything they share look like a J.Crew catalog? Ask yourself, are they human or robots? Because humans have bad days occasionally. This is likely all a carefully curated persona for social media. So why are you letting it make you feel bad about yourself?

3. Don't give a Fuck about people's opinions—especially people you would never want their advice.

This is easier said than done, especially if you are open on social media. It's human nature to want to be liked, and when we get negative opinions or comments from people, it's natural to want to take it to heart. But the thing is, some people interject their opinions, and we should never give them the time of the day. These are people that we would NEVER lean on in a crisis. NEVER ask for their advice, and we don't even trust them, so why does their opinion of us matter? I also don't think family and friend's opinions should be as big a deal as we tend to make them. I get it; you love your family and friends and want them to love everything you're doing, but sometimes, we can hold back our true calling because of a loved one's opinion. Truthfully, I believe that your own opinion of yourself is the most important thing. Are you making yourself proud? Are you doing things that bring you joy and peace? If not, then revisit what you're doing. But when making decisions, ask yourself if you're doing this because it will make someone else happy, or will this make you happy? We have one life to live; live it for yourself, not others. You'll be at peace in a way you never imagined possible.

Section II:
Getting to know yourself + strengthening your self-love and confidence muscles.

Chapter 6
Who the hell am I?

Something you should know about me is that I'm obsessed with the show Gilmore Girls. Honestly, I wish I had kept track of how many times I watched the series because, spoiler alert, it is probably at least 75 times. I saved my money in college to buy all of the seasons on DVD (for all my young folks, the things that played movies and TV shows before streaming existed) at a secondhand store. Having constant access to this series was EVERYTHING! Now that I can press play on Netflix at any time, you better believe that I STILL rewatch it as if I couldn't nearly recite the dialogue word for word by now. There was one episode in particular where Lorelei was seated at the kitchen table tasting and trying various flavors of Pop-Tarts, trying to decide if she actually liked them. She says to her daughter, Rory, "What if I don't like what I like because I like it, but because my mother doesn't like it and doesn't want me to like it, so that makes me like it?" This was an existential crisis of whether her whole life and all her interests were things she liked or whether her desire to rebel against her mother was why she liked these things. The age-old questions, what do I like, and who the hell am   I?

We can all admit we've pondered these questions a time or two. How could we not? It is easy to move through life on autopilot: wake up, work, dinner, relax, repeat. It is easy to get caught up in the day-to-day "to-do's," before you know it, a year has passed, and you think, "Where did this year go?" If you've ever been driving and suddenly think, "how did I even make it home?" because you were on autopilot the entire drive, (honestly that is always so scary, because HOW?) In this same sense, we can wake up one day, much like Lorelei Gilmore, not having any idea of who we are or what we actually like. I know because it happened to me. I'd also bet at some point in your life, it's happened to you, or maybe now you realize you don't have a damn clue of who you are. It's okay, friend; we're in this together, promise.

After that guy dumped me—I know he's getting a lot of publicity in this book, which is kind of annoying for me, but truly it was such a learning experience, I can suck it up—I realized I didn't have a clue of who Dani was or what made her happy. I remember buying the book "The Five Love Languages" and going to a local park, sitting and reading this book, wandering around, taking in nature, the flowers, the smells, and just spending time with myself.

It was LIBERATING. The only time I had felt like this was the semester I spent living abroad. At that time of my life, I was 20 years old and in a foreign country, living with a random family and surrounded by people who did not speak English or understand American culture. It took me a minute, or a hundred, to assimilate; once I did, however, it was life-changing. That trip was my first experience of traveling solo, having meals solo, and learning to spend time with just me. After quite some time, I had settled into the beauty of spending time in my own company, and I loved it. I would sit at a cafe outside, people-watching, sipping my coffee, eating a delicious pastry, reading a book, or writing in my journal. It was luxurious being content in my own space and doing the simplest things that made me happy. In fact, I became so comfortable with alone time that I even booked a bus ticket and traveled to a beach town a few hours away to enjoy a weekend alone, soaking up the sun. I stayed in a hostel, took myself to dinner and a glass of wine, and spent the weekend reading at the beach. I still remember that I was reading Harry Potter; that's how pivotal a moment it was! I even pulled the straps of my swimsuit all the way down and let the girls get some sun! It was only a brief moment; at that time, I had NOT done all the work I had now, but maybe it is time to go back to a topless beach!

When was the last time you did anything for you? Something that made you feel like yourself and that brought you pure joy?

When I was a kid, I wanted to spend ALL of my time doing the things I loved. I was constantly trying new activities, spending hours swimming, building forts, playing with dolls, playing sports, dancing, riding bikes, you name it. My friends and I would spend hours and hours riding our bikes or rollerblading—we didn't have cell phones back then—and honestly, we had no end goal in sight but to ride and have fun together. At some point, our priorities shifted once we hit high school. As so many of us do, we started living a life for other people, our innate sense of being slowly disappearing without even recognizing it.

I grew up thinking feeling like the only option after high school was attending college, I never imagined a different path. While there is nothing wrong with these expectations, I think it subconsciously becomes another layer in losing ourselves to please others. Regardless of your gender, you have had some kind of expectations instilled into you. While I can't say much from the male perspective, I can imagine that many men are expected to be strong, not show emotion, be the protector, and provide, while females are typically expected to be docile, kind, and great caretakers. All of these things are innately about pleasing others, not ourselves. In that respect, it makes sense how we tend to slowly lose ourselves as we age.

In my romantic relationships, I can now say that I was also trying to fit into these roles and to please my partner. The women in my life growing up were caretakers. My grandmother, the grand master caretaker, and my mom, her second in command. These women are two of the MOST selfless humans I've ever met. Both of their homes are immaculate; they'll both disagree, but they are. Growing up, I watched my mom clean the house, do the laundry, carpool, cook, and literally take care of everything. I thought that was what all women did, so naturally, when I moved in with my ex, I started assuming some of those responsibilities.

Laundry —I was already doing my own laundry—I can do yours too. I would be doing grocery shopping regardless; I'll just grab more. Cooking- I always cooked when I lived alone, so let's keep at it. I did all of this, as well as cleaned and decorated. It was fine, but I remember I was so annoyed, especially once our relationship started getting rocky. We had different work schedules, and with me having a more traditional 8-5 schedule and he and his friends having more night hours, they would come to our house, which was always the party house. Watching the game house (and there was ALWAYS a game), poker or game night house, and with all of that, they would stay up drinking and playing until the wee hours of the night. I would go to bed later than I wanted and be alone, laying there trying to sleep through the noise, only to wake up the next day to a mess. I tried so hard to be the perfect girlfriend, the chill girlfriend, and I ended up resenting him for it. Once, I mentioned how I seemed to do everything around the house, and he simply responded, " I never asked you to." Fuck. He was right.

In continued attempts to be super girlfriend, I became interested in everything he was interested in. I realize I have done this in every single relationship. Obsessed with sports, I'll watch every game with you, learn the players, rock the clothes, and even buy tickets to games for you for your birthday or Christmas. I would conform to their lifestyle, staying up later than I wanted to, drinking too much, sleeping through my alarm and not working out, or getting my morning routine done. I look back and know how dumb this all was, but I think we are all a little guilty of this as women. We've all either been the friend or had a friend who semi-disappear from life once they're in a new relationship. The ones that *always* need to spend time with their significant others, want to do all the couple things, bring them along to girl's dinners, and slowly aren't as available anymore. HELLO…. this is a huge part of losing our innate sense of self. When we twist ourselves into this perfect little girlfriend or wife box, we forget the activities, the music, the movies, the food, and the people that *actually* bring us joy and happiness.

I'm still no relationship expert, and I question WTF I'm doing regularly and if I am, in fact, the problem (I'm not the problem). I know I'm the MF prize, and now and instead of constantly trying to be the chill girl, I will be authentically myself. I no longer fake interest in things I don't give a fuck about, and I am not available 24/7 because I must prioritize my self-care, my friends, and hobbies that I enjoy, and if they don't like that, then on to the next one. I've also stopped trying to do girlfriend shit for men I'm not in a relationship with. It's not a game, it's just allowing myself to be treated like the damn prize I am, and once we've established mutual attraction and gone out several times; then maybe I'll consider cooking dinner for us. I don't need to prove my worth and value on the first few dates by cooking a home-cooked meal. I barely know you yet, and it's not my purpose in life to be a caretaker-especially to a man I'm only beginning to date.

These are simply my experiences, but I know so many others exist. Women who become mothers and, with the hustle and bustle of raising kids, completely wrap their identity in their family, only to wake up once they have an empty nest to be blindsided about their purpose in life now. We ALL have instances and experiences that have made us feel like we've lost ourselves. But just because we may have lost ourselves doesn't mean that it's forever. We can always find our way back, relearn, and learn what truly makes us tick. The most remarkable thing about this journey is that we never know what we will find that makes us feel like us again, that makes us understand and know who the F we are.

For me, one of the things I did was launch a new dance style class that was authentically me, focusing on unleashing our inner sexy and boosting our confidence. Twerking in front of a room of women was *never* on my life vision board, but it was life-changing. This led me to start teaching girls' night-in-chair dance classes, and

I even joined a burlesque class where I performed in a club and ended up, as you guessed it, in pasties and a thong. Talk about a way to figure out who the hell I was. But here is the thing: we deserve to know ourselves. We deserve to have an identity that is not based on outside factors. We deserve to spend some time doing things that bring us joy. Regardless of where you are, you can figure out who you are and make time to find yourself, and I'm going to give you a guideline on how to do so.

Tips for finding yourself:

1. *Revisit favorite hobbies from childhood (or young adulthood).*

Think back on your childhood or adolescence. What activity could you spend all day doing? You know, like how I mentioned earlier about riding my bike or rollerblading with my friends. What was your version of that? Before life got busy and we grew self-conscious, when we filled our days with things we got to do instead of things we had to do. It's okay if you still don't have the same love for that hobby. I'm still trying to see if my ankles can handle rollerblading; they've been sprained too many times since I used to cruise the streets. But you get what I mean. Maybe it's something you loved doing as a teenager or in early college. Personally, I forgot how much I enjoyed wandering around art museums. I did it when I studied in Europe—they are lousy with museums—and also something I enjoyed doing with my aunt. When I started getting to know myself again, I went solo to our local art museum and wandered around. It was weird at first, but I slowly eased into it without having a time constraint, anyone waiting for me, asking my opinion, or having any expectations of me whatsoever. I spent more time in front of paintings than I would have if I had companions. I even let emotions come up, and tears come to my eyes. It was magical and another piece of the puzzle of who the hell was Dani. Just think back to something you used to love and start there. See what happens and keep trying until you find something that sparks joy in your heart.

2. *Think of something you could do for hours without looking at the clock.*

 For me, this was always reading. I was the epitome of a book nerd. I'm talking about checking out six books from the library for our summer drive to Florida; kind of a book nerd. But when I went to college and started that long-term relationship, I didn't read nearly as much as I had in the past. I forgot how much I loved it and quickly reinstated my library card and got to it. Not only with fiction but with personal development books, (more on that later). But truly, I could sit outside or curl up in a blanket for hours, completely consumed in the faraway lands or whatever the novel's plot may be. For you, maybe it's painting, knitting, or gardening. Think of something you would spend half a day doing if time were not a hindrance. This will help expose you to all those things you enjoy and make you, you.

3. *What is something you've always wanted to do?*

Have you always wanted to learn another language? Take music lessons? Skydive? Plant a garden? Take a dance class? What is something you've said for years and years you wanted to do but have never actually done? DO IT. I'm telling you, it will not only boost your confidence, but it's going to make your inner child beam with pride. I told you already donning the homemade pasties, and becoming Cha Cha Cabernet in a burlesque show filled my creativity cup and confidence bucket more than I ever could have predicted. I've also taken a pole dancing class, a stilettos class, a Mandarin Chinese class, got a yoga certification, and the biggest one—moved to a beach town. Do something off your list of "want to's."

4. Notice when you do things out of obligation (or to please others).

We can't truly be in tune with ourselves if we're too busy managing other people's feelings. If we say yes to others out of obligation, we are saying no to ourselves. I know this can feel blasphemous to a people pleaser, but I promise, it's important. I started noticing this when I would be exhausted after a long week of work and feel like I had to say yes to my friends to go to the bars or dinner. All I wanted to do was order food and watch a movie on my couch. I used to come up with excuses to avoid going out, but the biggest change was simply learning to say no. I'd say, "I can't tonight," or "Thanks for inviting me, but tonight doesn't work." Or if they're close friends, I'd simply say, "I'm exhausted, and all I want to do is watch a movie and go to bed. Have fun, and I'll see you next time." Saying yes to others means saying no to ourselves.

5. *Spend 1 hour each week finding yourself.*

When you're starting to find out who the hell you are, you HAVE to make the time (because you never have!). Start with one hour a week. You can find it. This is your "you" time. This is not selfish; this is necessary. If you have an iphone, you can easily find out how much time you spend weekly on social media and other apps; take an hour from one of the mindless doom scrolling sessions. Finding yourself, knowing yourself, and honoring your needs allows you to be an even better woman, friend, wife, mother, sister, daughter, colleague, etc. If you're a parent, it also shows your children that prioritizing "me" time is important. And if you're dating or committed, it allows you to have an identity outside your relationship. This is healthy. Start with an hour, and then increase it gradually. Most of all, ENJOY!

Chapter 7
Feeling the feelings

I believe there are two types of people; those who need to express all their feelings to someone (and can open up easily), and others who prefer to be the ear to listen to those people (so they don't have to open up). I've always been the latter. Call me Dr. Dani, the unlicensed therapist, because my office hours are open—especially if that means I can divert any attention away from my feelings. I will listen to your problems and your struggles. You can call me to vent, cry, or scream; if you want advice, I got you. I can be an understanding and empathetic listener in times of need. This was part of my identity for a long time. I'm good at it; I'm naturally an empath. One of the reasons I have been successful in sales—is because I get to know people and make them feel comfortable and seen. It is a trait of mine I really value, yet it also can, at times, be my downfall. In my sales job, I divert all my attention to you, let you talk about yourself, your work, your family, your pastimes, and your opinions, and I'll smile, nod and respond. This helps build rapport and trust and ultimately builds a relationship so you will not think twice when it's time to make a purchase; you'll buy from me because you know and trust me. But it's also how I can be in my personal life. If I don't feel like talking about myself or being vulnerable, I will constantly divert the conversation back to the other person and let them talk about themselves. As I have already admitted, I struggle with vulnerability. I struggle with opening up and letting people see Dani's innermost feelings. I've been like this for as long as I can remember. Expressing emotions and feeling emotions is not my strong suit. I don't like to rely on others, and I am hyper-independent. I get frustrated when people are super needy and take an eternity to tell a story with excessive detail, I lose interest and desperately just want them to get to the point. When people are extra clingy, I tend to run, and because I've been cheated on in a romantic relationship, it's tough to earn my trust. (No wonder I'm single, eh?) I've done A LOT, and I mean A LOT of work, but I'm still not done.

I'm really not sure where my tendency to avoid expressing emotions came from and why it's so damn challenging to be vulnerable, but I have a few ideas. Growing up, my parents were still married; they were great parents, and I have amazing childhood memories. They did the best they could, and I don't blame them for anything at all. This is just me as an adult, looking back into my past for answers, patterns, and the root of these tendencies. My parents were eight years apart; my mom was 25 when I was born. She moved out of her parent's house at 18 and started her independent life. When I think of myself at 25, I can't imagine the responsibility of having a child. I think my mom is a badass. I admire her in so many ways, but we didn't always get along. I can look back now and understand. She was a young mother, and four years after I was born, my brother came along. Mom worked full-time, coordinated my brother's and my schedules, cooked dinner, packed lunches, signed all the permission slips, kept on us for doing homework, cleaned, woke up, and did it all over again. My dad was the fun one—he was like a big kid and left all the responsibility and disciplining to my mom. I can see now just how hard that must have been. I surely didn't make it any easier during my teenage years. If you're into astrology, I'm an Aries, and my mom is a Sagittarius. We are fire signs through and through, and boy, did we clash. We both have quick tempers and are stubborn. But growing up, before I developed any of that, I saw how quick my mom was to get angry, yell, storm off, slam doors, and be mad. When she and my dad fought, or she was in a particularly bad mood, I would stay in my room or another room waiting for it to stop. I learned to gauge my conversations based on her moods. And I know she didn't mean any of this, and I feel awful even writing this down because I love her so much, and we have a great relationship. But I do think this contributed to me shutting down my feelings.

My dad's family is boisterous and loud, fighting to be the center of attention. They always had to outdo each other, and it was fun watching them put on what felt like a show to me. If my dad's siblings were fighting, they would just stop calling each other and avoid everyone. My mom's family would argue passive-aggressively or hold their tongue until someone exploded and an argument commenced. Somewhere along the line, I learned that there wasn't room for my emotions, so I kept them to myself. That has continued into my adult life. But here's the thing: your emotions don't just evaporate; you have to feel them, or if not, you find a way to suppress them, and the only way I have found to suppress them is to numb them.

As a teenager and young college student, my numbing style of choice was food. We've talked about this already, but food was my friend. It comforted me, made me feel good in the moment, and filled me with excess. Excess was the ultimate goal because then I could shift my focus on feeling the misery of stomach aches and regret, leaving no space for other feelings. I was out of control with eating. I remember once craving donuts. Naturally, I drove up to the local donut shop, and when the smells and flavors provoked me, I couldn't decide which one I wanted. So, I got a half dozen donuts, intending to take them home to share with my family, but as soon as

I got in my car, it was like I became possessed by the donuts and had to eat one immediately, or I would die. By the time I had driven a mile, I had already devoured 3 donuts. I could not let my family know how many donuts I had eaten, so I ended up eating the rest of the donuts, parking at a park, crying over what I had just done, and disposing of the evidence in the parking lot trash can. I never shared my problems, never felt the feelings, and just coasted by on the trail of sugar and shame. I wish this were the only time something like this happened, but it wasn't.

At another point in my life, I used male attention and sex to numb my feelings. Yet again, it's not something I'm proud of but part of what made me who I am. I was so desperate not to feel lonely, hurt, betrayed, and worthless that I sought attention from men. If a man wanted to sleep with me, it made me feel less lonely and unworthy. However, relying solely on sex to feel worthy or less lonely only made me feel even more unworthy and lonely— the math didn't add up as I hoped. I would match with people on dating apps to boost my ego, with no intention of meeting them. My previous experiences with sex had only been with people I truly cared about and either were in a relationship with or were building a relationship with. Naive interactions with men made me realize I could be a player just like them. Meeting someone, feeling instant chemistry, having one-night stands, and then leaving, never to talk to them again. But all this ever did was make me feel good at the moment, only to wake up feeling lonely and, at times, regretful.

Booze. We've had quite a relationship, booze and I. I've given it up for lent (even though I'm not catholic, I like giving something up), countless sober Octobers, dry January's. I've even gone nearly a year without booze. Yet, like a toxic ex, it lures me back in. As an adult, alcohol has become my numbing agent of choice. It has been bad. Let's say that many of the aforementioned one-night stands have happened due to the loosening properties of alcohol. I've made some decisions under the influence that I would NEVER in a million years make sober. I've started fights, almost ruined friendships, embarrassed myself to no end, woke up not knowing where I was, and had more hangover shame spirals than I can ever tell you. Yet, when I found out my dad was diagnosed with Alzheimer's, I really started relying more heavily on booze to numb everything. I will have to give the full story here for you to understand, and well, it's not pretty.

My dad started experiencing more moments of forgetfulness. Initially, we thought he was just being lazy or not thinking clearly, but then he started leaving his wallet at the gas station or Walmart, putting things back in odd places, and acting "off". At that point, he was 57, and I was 25, living with my boyfriend at the time, and we partied a lot. Sure, I sometimes overindulged, but I wasn't drinking excessively alone—just at parties or when we went out, which was often. After my mom, frustrated with the lack of answers from various doctors who diagnosed him with things like 'depression,' was finally referred to a memory center. That's when the word 'Alzheimer's' was mentioned, and our world shifted forever. My dad, who was always the life of the party and a kid at heart, had Alzheimers, and I, a daddy's girl, was devastated. But the diagnosis wasn't the hardest part; it was the next 10 years of our lives that were. This is where booze became much more of a friend than I like to admit.

It started with me drinking more when we went out, or wanting to take more shots, drinking more of the bottle of wine, staying up later than I should, drinking with friends who mostly all had restaurant jobs, whereas I had an 8-5. One night, I remember drinking entirely too much and, after trying to keep my feelings numbed, calling my brother hysterically crying about our dad. Not only did I not know how to process these intense emotions, I felt like I had to stay strong for my mom. She was, after all, the one caring daily for her husband, and I felt like I had to keep it together. I also started feeling like no one could possibly understand what I was dealing with. No one ever asked me to stay strong. My mom never said she couldn't also be there for me and my emotions. Still, my lifelong experience thus far of shielding my feelings deep inside prevented me from allowing people to really be there for me during this time. That feeling only got worse as my dad's condition inevitably declined.

I would go over to my parent's house and stay with my dad like a babysitter while my mom would run errands or very rarely, go to dinner with friends. Sometimes, it would be like nothing had ever changed with him besides a few repetitive conversations; other times, it would be all I could do to keep it together. Watching someone you love slowly lose themselves and literally disappear in front of your eyes is something you can never prepare yourself for. I started buying wine on the way home from their house, desperately needing to take off the edge in any way possible. Sometimes, I'd let myself cry as soon as I pulled out of their neighborhood, but still, I never opened up to anyone about what I was feeling. Drink, soothe, cry, drink, repeat. Here is the thing: You can only hold feelings in for so long before they come up to the surface and explode out of you, and they always do at the worst times.

I have a few, okay, a lot, of these instances. One of the last ones, the time I gave up booze for nearly a year, was a few months after my dad died. It had been a shitty day; my phone stopped working, I spent hours trying to fix it, drank a glass or 2 of wine to ease my frustration, and ended up at Verizon, where yet another iPhone had stopped working, and I had to replace without me actually wanting a new phone. (This was the third time something like this had happened, but I'm also too lazy to learn how to use a non-iPhone, so here we are). One of my closest friends was having a party. All their friends and family were going to be there, and it was essentially a last hoorah before her family moved to Arizona for her husband's new military orders. I didn't want to go before the phone fiasco had started. There are days I just don't have it in me, or I feel upset for no reason or have social anxiety, and being anywhere but home alone feels like an uphill battle I want nothing to do with. I knew where my mental space was that day, and I knew I should have stayed home—but I went because I felt obligated; I didn't want to bail or flake. I did the exact opposite of what I advise you to do. Like I said, I'm still a work in progress. Immediately, they all started wanting to feed me drinks and shots, because until I reach a certain level, drunk Dani is the life of the party, she is a good time. Before I knew it, after not eating anything most of the day, I was blacked out and sitting in the front yard alone, sobbing, crying over my dad, and begging to go home. I will never forget waking up in my friend's bed, somehow in pajamas that weren't mine, head pounding, stomach-turning, and knowing I had to get out of there. Talk about shame.

I'm still not perfect. Sometimes, I still think maybe I should break up with alcohol once and for all. I still use it like a crutch at times. But unlike in the past, I journal it all out and don't shame myself. I give myself grace and acknowledge that I'm only human. I've been in therapy, I've tried not drinking, and I've tried drinking, yet the grief of my dad's illness doesn't go away. It does get easier with time to talk about him without wanting to cry. I can share memories and smile or laugh, but I still fall apart sometimes. Deep down, I know that even if it wasn't Alzheimer's, I'd feel the same. But there's something about that disease and what I witnessed that is different from someone who perhaps had cancer. Grieving someone who is still alive is nonsensical; it defies logic. Watching someone waste away in a hospital bed where they have to be taken care of like a toddler—diaper changed, hand fed, out of sorts 99% of the time—is not something anyone should witness.

Walking into your parent's home with your dad dead in a hospital bed in the living room is also not something that someone should ever experience. I had a lot of anger; I still do in some ways. I was bitter for a long time, feeling like no one could ever understand how I felt. They couldn't imagine, and I was pissed. I didn't open up to hardly anyone. Honestly, I was annoyed when my friends and family did ask me about my dad because they would get that look of pity or make a comment of "I can't imagine," which still infuriated me. (Sidenote- using the phrase "I can't imagine" is not the move. If you really tried, you could imagine, you don't want to. I know we aren't taught what to say in these situations, but believe me when I say that "I can't imagine" makes it about you, which is not what the person going through the thing you cannot imagine wants to hear.). The thing is, I know that everyone is well-intentioned; not a single one of us knows how to handle these uncomfortable and delicate situations best. I can understand that now, looking back. However, it made me want to open up even less. I would just lie and say, "I'm fine." "Hanging in there." "Surviving." It was easy, and most people believed me, or at least thought they had fulfilled their duty enough and didn't ask any further questions. (Thank God). My dad's family mostly stayed away, not dealing with it—are we surprised at all of my avoidant tendencies? My mom's family was a huge support system, yet they, at times, would start to cry or say how unfair it was or how young my mom was to deal with all of this. It was hard to ever feel like anyone could acknowledge my specific grief, and I know how incredibly selfish that sounds, but it's true. This entire time was the most isolating time of my life. I felt like part of me also died. Sometimes, I still do.

Regardless of the numbing agent, the feelings remain. If we leave them never to be dealt with, they metastasize into something far worse. Maybe your numbing agent is work, maybe its drugs, maybe its social media. Whatever it is, avoidance doesn't make it disappear. Unresolved trauma and grief truly can make us sick. If you have never read the book, "The Body Keeps Score" by Bessel Van Der Kolk, I would recommend it. As the title suggests, the body does keep score of our trauma. Whether we numb it or not, it lingers there underneath the surface. Believe me, I know feeling the feelings SUCKS! But its time to choose which sucks less; reliving the same feelings over and over and over; possibly breaking down at the most random time because you've never processed your grief, or crying until it feels like there can't possibly be any tears left, talking through the feelings and moving forward. We can do hard things. If I, the avoidant, vulnerability allergic, numbing extraordinaire, can work on this, so can you.

Nonexpert advice on feeling the feelings:

1. *Therapy.*

Look, I didn't grow up in a household or in a time when therapy was normalized. I've shared how not vulnerable I have been most of my life. The idea of opening up to a stranger gave me anxiety. I also felt like it meant that there was something wrong with me—honestly, there was- but it doesn't have to mean anything bad. Therapists are trained to deal with complex emotions and to help you do the same. Therapy helped me immensely, and I think we can all benefit from it. I'll never forget the day I logged onto a call, expecting a woman therapist, only to log in to zoom to see a younger black man staring at me, introducing himself as my therapist. I was so confused and thought about switching therapists, but honestly, having someone so different from me opened my eyes and mind to ideas that I likely never would have had if it were a white woman like myself. Therapy helped me learn to be vulnerable with a stranger. It forced me not to divert the conversation away from me. I was FORCED to sit in my uncomfortableness, process it and learn ways to manage. Truly a game-changer.

2. *Find your support system.*

Maybe therapy isn't for you. If that is the case, find someone that you can trust. It can be a good friend, family member, mentor, minister… find someone. Not everyone deserves access to our innermost feelings. I think there is still a balance between completely shutting down emotionally and being an oversharer. Not everyone, even our closest friends and families, can always give us that sense of comfortability to open up, and that is okay. I worked on being vulnerable with a good friend who was my "newest" friend at the time. Her ability to be vulnerable and share her experience of losing her dad with me gave me the space and peace to confide in her. A shared experience and empathy can go a long way. Someone who will let you share your truth without making it about them, simply being present and acknowledging you and validating your feelings—that is what we all need. Thank you, Emily.

3. *Journal*.

I grew up writing all my feelings, but somewhere along the way, I stopped. Perhaps this is when I really began numbing instead of processing (hmm). Brain-dumping your feelings, though on paper, gets them out of your head and closer to being felt. Sometimes, I look back at what I have written and notice patterns which show me my true feelings or maybe even present what is wrong. If we don't spend time with our feelings, how do we truly know ourselves? It's weird at first to write to ourselves. When you first start, it may be really menial thoughts, but once you get loose and feel more comfortable, you'll be pleasantly surprised at how powerful the simple task of free writing can be.

4. *Talk about things slowly but more frequently.*

I started sharing a few things in small bites with strangers. Actually, saying the words that my dad had died or my dad was battling Alzheimer's started to make it more real, and the more I shared, the more comfortable I became in doing so. It sounds weird, but saying things out loud to other people instead of living in my own little world of pain made it easier to acknowledge my feelings. The more we do this in little bite sizes, the easier it gets and the more we work on our vulnerability. If you're sweating already thinking about this, maybe take an even smaller step, but do try my love.

5. *Cry.*

Just freaking cry. I held back tears for years in the name of being strong, but there is nothing more cathartic than crying. I don't do it often in front of people. I'm trying to be better at that. I still find myself holding back and having a stoic-like presence in front of others, so if I feel the tears start to come when I'm around people who support me, I'll let them come out. But sometimes, I listen to songs I know that will make me cry, and I'll just lay in my bed with my headphones and cry it out. Its a way to feel the feelings and let them go and also to release all the pent-up tears I never allowed to fall. If you hold on to the tears, I promise they will come out at some point, and likely in the most unfortunate time, hello, blackout drunk crying in the grass (not a fine moment at all *facepalm*).

Chapter 8
Busting through your comfort zone

I wasn't always someone who enjoyed, or even ever actually did things that weren't familiar or comfortable, in fact, I avoided it altogether. Give me what I know, and don't force me to do anything I'm unsure of. That was how I could control the situation and have some level of confidence. The idea of venturing outside of my comfort zone made me want to break out into hives immediately. Growing up, I didn't see a lot of examples of getting out of the comfort zone. Our family and my friend group did not do things alone. In fact, my aunt would suggest things she wanted to do but then complain that she didn't have anyone to do them with. The idea of doing those things by herself never crossed her mind. I learned that in order to go on trips, dinners, museums, or any kind of event in public, you needed company. I'll never forget when I decided to study in Spain for a semester, and my grandparents acted as if I would be living in a war zone. In their minds, they could not comprehend why I would want to live abroad. Little did I know this experience was where I would start to edge up against my comfort zone.

Have you ever gone to dinner by yourself? A movie or a vacation? If not, why? Really think about the reason you feel uncomfortable doing things alone because I hate to break it to you (but clearly, that's what I do here); the answer is the root of your lack of confidence, my friend. The foundation of confidence is built on feeling comfortable in your own skin. The more time you spend in your own company and out in the world without depending on anyone else, the more your confidence will soon grow. It's all interconnected, don't you see? I've had friends and family who could never fathom the idea of getting food alone or even going to a movie alone (to me, that is the easiest place to start because you're in the dark in a room where no one is talking!) This lack of comfort alone says more about your own relationship with yourself than anything, and I learned this all too well.

My mom and I were talking once about this topic, and she told me a powerful story that really made her second-guess things.

One night after work, she had gone to dinner by herself. She had been craving a certain kind of food and went to get said food, deciding to eat at the restaurant. When she came home, her mom asked where she had been; after relaying that she'd been at dinner, her mother inquired, with who? To which my mom replied that she had gone alone. Completely taken aback, her mother began making comments about what other people thought seeing her eating alone, and how she couldn't believe she went by herself. She said to my mom "I could NEVER do that." This conversation made my mom begin to overthink her actions, questioning and doubting her choices and believing that perhaps she had done something wrong and maybe people *did* think she was some lonely loser eating alone. None of these thoughts had ever crossed her mind, yet with one opinion, she doubted herself and told me that following that moment, she had never again dined alone.

As a woman, I sometimes feel it can be more taboo, societally speaking, to dine alone, whereas men often belly up to the bar, grab a beer and food, proceeding to watch the game with no issues, no self-doubt, no weirdness. Women, on the other hand, don't do this often. I challenge you to try it. See what it feels like to take yourself out to dinner. You don't have to grab a table; maybe ease into it all by starting at the bar. If you drink, loosen up with some liquid courage. I will never forget one of the periods I was sober curious, and practicing abstaining. I had taken a solo trip to check out a potential city I was considering moving to. Sitting at the bar alone and not drinking was overwhelming as if the booze made it more acceptable for some reason, and I found myself heavily relying on my cell phone to feel less weird. It's baby steps; at least I was out there, right? Bring a book with you to give your mind something to focus on. Getting out of your comfort zone doesn't have to be a grand ordeal. Dipping a toe out of that zone is reason for celebration. Let me tell you a few other personal stories, some bigger and others smaller, to give you some ideas.

By now, y'all know my history with any issues regarding my body. I hid it, covered it in shapewear, wore long shirts and one-piece bathing suits, and never considered doing anything else. As I started to heal my relationship with myself, I started to test the waters with more revealing clothing. First was the bikini—even after losing weight, I was terrified— and it took a pep talk. I would see other people smaller than me wearing full-coverage swimsuits and think that they were clearly making fun of and judging me for being this size and showing more skin. That first bikini time, I was the thinnest I had ever been in my adult life, and yet I still refused to wear a body-hugging dress without Spanx. I did not care if it was a million degrees outside; I had to force my body to appear smaller by any means necessary. I got the courage to wear a body con dress, and despite it being hot AF in Miami, I would only wear this skin-tight dress if I was squished into Spanx. I'm not opposed to Spanx or any kind of shapewear, but let's be honest, in the summer, it makes you that much hotter, and let's not even talk about trying to pee with these things on, even with the open crouch of Spanx, it takes some effort not to pee all over yourself.

Several years later, and many pounds heavier, I've started wearing crop tops, despite being heavier, despite being older, almost in spite of everything. I remind myself constantly of how long I covered myself up, and it is no longer acceptable if I want to wear a cute crop and you can see my stretch marks, my rolls, the FUPA in my jeans, so fucking be it! I still, at times, feel self-conscious, but this version of Dani honors young Dani, who hated herself so badly. I recently, at 37, went to a concert in Atlanta where I wore short black jean shorts and a crop top. Now, it sounds so damn simple, right? But if you only knew that at this point, the crop top for me was only worn mostly with athletic shorts because, let's face it, jeans put the FUPA on display. I did the damn thing with the encouragement of a great girlfriend; thanks, Jordan, and honestly, I look at the pictures and think how cute I look! Not that I need external validation, but that night, I had several men hollering at me, trying to get my number, so it's not like the stretch marks and FUPA hindered their interest. And that is the thing, my friends, we think people are thinking of us as negatively as we think of ourselves, that they are judging us, but newsflash, they are NOT thinking about us. They're in their own minds thinking of themselves, period. So why give strangers opinions who don't give a F about us the power to allow us to hide or not wear what we actually want to? Listen up sis, if you've ever wanted to rock a crop top, a short skirt, or whatever… DO IT NOW and rock the shit out of it with your bad self!

If a crop top and bikini were tame for you, let's discuss the Korean spa. Have you ever been? I remember studying abroad, I had a friend or two mention going to a bathhouse, and I listened to them while silently thinking there was NO way you'd ever catch me in one. Fast forward many years, and I walked into a Korean spa. Never say never, I suppose.

We paid our entrance fee and were given our spa outfits— which, by the way, orange is not the best color as we all looked like inmates— and we made our way to the dressing room. I thought maybe we'd start with the saunas, these you enjoyed in your prison clothes, and it would maybe ease me into the actual baths and the whole getting naked business; instead, we ripped that band-aid right the fuck off. My friend, Jordan, who had convinced me to try the spa, loves being naked, so she was here for it and had experienced Korean spas before. Having spent the majority of my adult life avoiding looking at my naked body and only slowly beginning to accept and be more comfortable with nudity, I was intimidated AF.

Let me set the scene; there were naked women everywhere. Walking through the locker room, standing and having conversations with the workers fully nude, this was the first minute for me after turning the corner into the locker room. Walking over to my locker, where I would have to leave behind all my clothing, they handed me a towel that was basically a large hand towel, and I could walk and let it cover my vagina or my boobs, but nothing else. As I started to undress, I looked at my friend and said, "Girl, you are really getting me out of my comfort zone right now; whew, lord." I'm not the kind of girl who ever gets naked in front of anyone besides someone I'm being intimate with or the doctor. This was going to be something else.

Before you can get into any of the baths, you must shower; for me, it was not only washing off my sweat and dirt but my shame. The showers were separated by glass partitions but had no door, so you were on display to everyone in the baths and anyone walking by. I honestly can't even describe the feeling I felt in this situation. I was still trying to hide myself, not caring if someone saw my butt, but so nervous about having the front side of my body on display. We made our way to the first bath, me holding my hand towel strategically covering my vagina, and I eased my way into the bath. Settling in, feeling the warmth of the water, and watching as my boobs floated up (if only they stayed that high and perky, okkkaay!) I took a deep breath and began to settle. We tried multiple baths, a cold plunge, two different saunas, an infrared light, and even a body scrub—again, full the fuck on display laying on a massage table in a room with eight other women, getting scrubbed the hell down.

It took me some time to feel comfortable, but ultimately, with the help of Jordan, I realized we are all just a body. Read that again. You are just a body- we all have a body. It's only the outside casing of who we are, period. Seeing women of all ages, all sizes, ethnicities, and backgrounds enjoying their natural form in front of other women was empowering. It made me realize that it is society that teaches us to feel insecure and shameful about our nudity. We all have imperfections, bumps, wrinkles, cellulite, and parts that gravity has affected more than others, but at the end of the day, our bodies only house our beautiful souls. We do not need to be ashamed of our forms. I see this experience as one of the most empowering experiences to date. And I can't believe I'm saying it, but, I'm looking forward to enjoying a Korean spa next time.

This last example of getting out of your comfort zone, and honestly, I'm not recommending it *unless* it is something you've always wanted to do, is moving away from your comfort zone. Less than a year ago, I did just that. I grew up as a water baby. We had a pool in our backyard, as did my grandparents. I remember the first time I was at the beach and looking out to the expanse of the ocean; it was love at first sight. As the years passed, the ocean has always been my happy place, the place that makes me feel at peace, the place where I can always find a grounded space. I dreamed of living near the water, and in southwest Ohio, the closest thing was the Ohio River. Let's just say it's not the same calming energy. I didn't pursue living near the ocean most of my life, but that desire stayed buried in me.

I had a great time at college, but part of me wishes I had gone out of state to a bigger city or the beach. But at 18, I wasn't ready, which I can admit now. It took until 20 years old to decide to spend a semester in Spain. Even that was tougher than I thought it would be at first. Still, I knew it was necessary to grow my language abilities. In fact, when I arrived in Spain alone, I thought, what in the actual fuck did I just get myself into? As I got older, I had the desire to move to a big city. Chicago was on my list, but I always found an excuse: money, not knowing anyone, not having a job there. Then I met my now ex and gave up that idea. Next, my dad was diagnosed with Alzheimer's. As he deteriorated, I realized there was no way I could, with any conscience, leave him or leave my mom to deal with things alone. I traveled but put the moving out-of-state dream on pause to be there to support my family, and I don't regret it whatsoever.

The pandemic happened, and while that was a whirlwind of a time, it did change the landscape of work as remote working became acceptable, and with that change, my goal re-emerged. My dad was literally on his deathbed, and with a new world opened where I could more easily work from my computer, I started thinking about that dream more and more often. They say when you can't get an idea out of your head, the universe is nudging you to make that happen. I wholeheartedly concur. After conversing with a good friend, Jordan, thank you again, about my desire to work remotely, she checked her network to realize she had a recruiter friend. Multiple company interviews later, I was offered a job to work in international finance from wherever I wanted. The dream was in motion. I'll tell you, when the road to your dream begins to be paved, it becomes exciting and simultaneously scary AF. I spent some time checking out various places in Florida. Growing up vacationing in Florida, I knew it would be a great first stop to see if I liked living outside Ohio and near the ocean. While Miami was in my heart, I knew it was not the place for me to live; I'd get into so much trouble with the access to partying 24/7. Even more so, I was concerned that all my work on accepting my body would really be tested in that environment. Looking into other places, I took a solo trip to Fort Meyers, and while I loved it, I knew it wasn't the place for me to move. Randomly, after a google search of the best places for singles in Florida, I ended up in northeast Florida (I don't believe this article whatsoever now that I live here for the record), spending a month in Jacksonville Beach. I loved it, but after a weekend of driving north to Amelia Island, I knew I had found something truly special.

It wasn't smooth sailing, this plan. I packed up the house I had been renting, put my belongings in storage, and spent a month in Jax Beach. The intention was to come back to Ohio for a month or two and then make the move permanently. I had a POD delivered to my mom's house to pick up my life and be sent to Jacksonville, intending to be in my new home within a few weeks. Let's just say that Hurricane Ian and the universe had other plans. I had put a deposit on renting a house I'd never seen. Timelines kept getting pushed back, and months later, I was finally able to visit that house in person. I hated it. Immediately, I had bad vibes; this could not be the place for me. It didn't feel right. I knew deep down in my gut. The house wasn't right, but being back on that island, I knew it was still the right place. I made it back to Ohio and signed a lease on an apartment sight unseen, rolling the dice that the universe would have my back. A few months later, my dog Layla and I had a Honda Civic full of our life belongings and were making the 13-hour drive towards our new life.

Once we got there, I spent most of the first few weeks getting organized and making my apartment feel like home. Once I was done with that work, I woke up and wondered what the fuck I had done. I was in a new state, a new town, where I knew absolutely no one, and I was scared as hell. It took some time, but I settled in. I met some friends, I found hobbies, I started dating a little, and I realized that I was going to be alright. Most weekends, I go to the beach for a few hours, relaxing, reading, and ultimately being in awe that this is my home. I often forget that I'm not on vacation and I, in fact, live in this magical place. I realize this is a drastic example of getting out of your comfort zone, but I will say that I've not felt more proud of myself for having a dream and achieving it. I've been here an entire year and have grown even more, and I feel like I've found a wonderful new home. Above all, betting on myself has been the best thing I've ever done, and that never would have happened if I had not gotten out of my comfort zone.

Here are my top tips for getting out of your comfort zone:

1. *Take a breath and jump.*

This doesn't have to be some big thing you take a jump on. It could be an Instagram post you're thinking of uploading; just take a breath and share. It could be setting up a dating profile and going on a first date. It doesn't have to be moving across the country or joining a burlesque troupe, but it needs to be something. If you never push yourself outside of your everyday routine, how do you expect to grow? Whatever it is that you want, just take a breath and dive in— you will never learn about yourself, how strong you are and what you could be unless you leap.

2. *Try something new.*

Try something different than what you know. A new fitness class, traveling, dining alone, starting a business, taking a business course, learning a new language, something outside of your normal. When we push outside of what is comfortable, we grow, and we realize how fucking amazing we are! Added bonus: Oftentimes you end up meeting cool people who share the same interests as you, score!

3.   *Do one thing that scares you*.

If you are scared of something, that means its worth it. This is a bigger test of faith, a bigger leap. What is that goal you've always wanted to achieve? What's the dream that's never left your soul? Do something that scares the hell out of you and gets you closer to that dream or goal. As I'm writing this book, I think, who the fuck am I to have the audacity to be writing this? How can I be an author? But guess what? Writing a book has always been a goal since I was a child, and it scared the shit out of me so badly that I never tried until now. Move the needle closer to the goal. Move past your fear. You're a bad ass bitch.

Chapter 9
Keeping promises to yourself

For the majority of my adult life, I set audacious, lofty, unattainable goals which I never kept. I would start so strong and so determined only to say fuck it and give up. It's no surprise that my confidence was in the toilet. I believed that what I lacked was motivation and discipline, and I thought I was just lazy and I could never stick to anything. After a while, I stopped sharing my goals with anyone; I never mentioned what new diet I was on or a new hobby I wanted to try out because, inside, I knew I'd just fail. How could someone not fail when they declared they were going to lose 50lbs in a couple of months by eliminating basically every food group and essentially surviving on air? Sure, let me never eat sugar, carbs, or junk food again and only drink water while I go out and watch friends enjoy cocktails. It's going to be so fun!!! I would go all or nothing, and as soon as I had one minor misstep outside of perfection, I would eat anything and everything in sight, further reinforcing my lack of willpower and diminishing my confidence.

These habits didn't exist only when it related to food and diet, but many other aspects. I have always been someone who is multi-passionate and has many great ideas along with ambition, but let's just say that the follow-through aspect is not my strong suit. What can I say? I get bored easily; I'm an Aries. Perhaps I also have undiagnosed ADD, but who knows? The crazy thing is that I have embodied this identity for the majority of my life. I used it almost like a shield or an excuse for when I'd inevitably bail on whatever the hobby or goal du jour was. It's only been in the last few years that I have proven to myself that this identity is no longer something that has to be mine. When I think of all the things I have started and never followed through with, it is kind of embarrassing.

Piano lessons to start with. I enjoyed them but didn't love the piano, so I stopped taking lessons (I can still remember Every Good Boy Does Fine and FACE, though, so it wasn't all in vain). I have always enjoyed writing, mostly simple poems or song lyrics. I had this vision of playing acoustic guitar covers and singing in coffee shops for fun. At this point in life, I had my license and a part-time job, and my mom said if I wanted guitar lessons, go for it, but I had to pay for lessons. I had an acoustic guitar my dad gave me, and I was excited to start this new venture. Of course, I was paired up with a young male teacher that I immediately developed a crush on, thanks universe. As my teenage hormones were raging, I was so attracted to men who played guitar; honestly, I've never grown out of that. There is just something about a man plucking the strings with his fingers that is sexy AF. In all seriousness, though, this man was hot *and* a talented teacher. We learned the basics, but each week, he would allow me to bring in a song I wanted to learn. So I'd bring in a CD of whatever song I was obsessed with at the moment, and he'd listen and learn on the spot to then teach me. I wasn't very good, but honestly, maybe I could have been. I enjoyed playing Nirvana and all my other, at the time, favorite emo bands' music. I stuck with it, even taking my guitar with me to college, but inevitably, like all things, I stopped. I keep saying at some point; I'm going to get rid of my long nails and re-learn how to play just to actually do a coffee shop or bar set so I can I finally say I've done it. Stay tuned.

If you truly want to increase your confidence, you have to start actually keeping promises to yourself. Every time you break your own word, your confidence diminishes. Think about it like this: you show up for your family, your friends, your coworkers, and your neighbors, right? If a family member called and asked you to go with them to a doctor's appointment, you'd go, right? Your friend calls begging you to go with them to a new fitness class. Would you join? If your partner asked you to be their plus one for a work function, you'd surely attend without a second thought. When your kids need supplies for a science project, or your neighbor needs help with a garage sale, or your coworker needs advice on how to approach your boss about a work issue, you would be there, wouldn't you? Without question, you show up for the important people in your life, so why can't you do the same for yourself? No, really, I am asking, this is not rhetorical. Reflect on this. Put the book down and write out your answer. Listen, I know I'm being tough, but this is how we do it around here. If you can't answer this question, then how can you grow your confidence?

I'll help you by giving you my answer, ok? After all, we're friends by this point, and this is what friends do. My reasoning was that I didn't think I was worthy. This is something I still reflect on, as it's difficult to imagine now why I didn't feel worthy because I know I am. Yet, there is still young Dani who didn't always feel worthy, who felt less than, who felt unseen, and for all those reasons, I always felt I didn't deserve to make myself proud or keep promises to myself. My reason may not resonate with you, and that's fine, but you must find a reason, sister. It will give you a point of reference when you can see yourself self-abandoning in the future.

A year ago, after abandoning a goal I had of finishing a yoga instructor training, I finally finished. I've taught dance fitness for years. I can teach a strength training class, chair class, or twerk class, but I wanted to do something to challenge my skills and get myself out of my fitness comfort zone. I've taken many yoga classes and love it. I think it's a beautiful mind/body connection that allows us to strengthen not only our bodies but our minds. When the pandemic hit, I came across an online yoga instructor training that you could complete at your own pace. Despite the higher cost, I invested in myself and was excited to start.

Like clockwork, though, I got bored. When I tell you that the yoga instructor training is time-consuming, it is 200 hours. Sections of anatomy, learning all the muscles of the body, the history of yoga, the asanas, how to sequence, the list goes on and on. It was overwhelming. I felt like I was making no progress. So I just stopped. A year later, I was so annoyed at myself, thinking how I had spent nearly $400 on this to only once again not complete it. I was embarrassed; I had told people I was doing this training, and had nothing to show for it.

I was embarrassed at my own lack of discipline. So, I did what I've always needed to do. I planned it the fuck out. I bought a dry-erase board calendar and mapped out how to finish the certification, taking it day by day. It took time; I had to erase my overzealous schedule when I couldn't keep up and rearrange the dates, but I finally got it done. The pride I felt in receiving that certification was intoxicating. I was proud enough at that point; it wouldn't have mattered if I never taught a yoga class. I was so thrilled at my achievement. But, adding actually leading my first class to my history is priceless. I realized accomplishing a goal is not about any potential money, titles, or accolades; its simply making myself proud.

This is how we ended up here, and you're reading these words now. I'm again proving myself wrong, and honestly, this has been one of the pillars of my growth, and I've proved that I don't have to identify with someone who has no follow-through. Since I fell in love with reading as a young girl, I've always had this bucket list idea in the back of my head to write a book. I didn't tell many people, and then I'd randomly say I want to write a book before I die, but with no other information. I never actually did anything to attempt to make this goal a reality; however, it was just something that stayed in the back of my head.

I started after college, on a whim, and wrote maybe 3 pages in a Word document, never to come back to it. Then, I'd write down a different plot idea, feel excited, and forget all about it. You get the picture. Before this book became an idea, I had actually written nearly 18 chapters of a fiction book (that I will finish because I believe in that trilogy), so I knew I was making progress and showing myself that, in fact, I had the ability. One day, out of nowhere, the idea of the book you are reading presented itself. Before I knew it, I was mapping out all the chapter titles and sections without hesitation, and it was like the words just effortlessly poured out of me. I knew, with that synchronicity, this would be my first book—the fitting words to make that bucket list idea of childhood Dani come to fruition. I've struggled and failed time and time again. I have written, erased, re-written, and re-planned out my goals to get the draft done countless times—thankfully, the dry-erase calendar board is easy to erase and start anew. No matter what, I have made progress, and that momentum has increased my confidence in my abilities and reaffirmed just how determined I am. This, my friend, is why keeping promises to yourself is so important; it can be positively life-changing.

Here are my tips for keeping promises to yourself:

1. *Just fucking do it.*

It sounds simple, but sometimes it's not. Habits run DEEP. Our brain is far too smart, and most of the time, it has YEARS of developing these neuropathways and finding proof that we disappoint ourselves time and time again. This is why I suggest to take a page out of Nike's book and Just Fucking Do It. This is the only way your brain can slowly develop new habits and, even more importantly, find new proof that it can in fact, keep its promises. Somedays, it sucks; you will grumble through it, still feel like a fucking failure, and be miserable, but you are building your confidence brick by MF brick—Tetris style. If you can take care of it now, just fucking do it, don't wait until later. Take a deep breath, grin and bear it for 30 minutes and get that shit done. Rinse and repeat. Before you know it, you may even smile while completing these promises that at some point, you'll be so fucking proud of yourself you'll almost forget what a shit show it was to get there.

2. *Plan it out.*

No one is surprised by this since I already eluded to my success, but get a blank calendar—whether you like a dry-erase board like me, or you're a pen to paper girlie, or you're a tech wiz, pick your poison.

Make a plan for the month—write out your goal (that is actually achievable) and maybe even a stretch goal to give you something to work towards. Once you have your month goal, plan it out day by day. It may seem tedious, but as you cross off the days, you build consistency, and you slowly reach the goal. It feels pretty amazing to see the progress, and breaking it out by the day makes it seem so much more achievable. Spoiler—it also helps build the new neuropathways in your brain, which means you are slowly building consistency and changing your old self. WIN/WIN!

3. *Reward yourself.*

Reward, bribe; tomato, *tomahto*. For real, though, if you are motivated by rewards, try it. If your goal is to work out 3 days a week, then maybe after a month of following through, you reward yourself with a new workout outfit or tennis shoes. Goal to learn Spanish, and you take lessons every week for a month, and you even meet a new Spanish-speaking friend to practice with, book a massage or a even better, a trip to practice those new skills IRL. If you're motivated by money, maybe you take $100 and put it away. If you meet your goal at the end of the month, you can use it for whatever you want. And if you fail, you have to donate it. Figure out what motivates you and make it happen. You got this.

Chapter 10

The subtle art of saying no

Two letters, N.O. So simple to pronounce, yet it can be so challenging to actually say. Admittedly, it was not a major part of my vocabulary for many years. Maybe it was my tendency to want to people please, or perhaps, the fact as women, we are taught we should be agreeable, supportive, selfless, caring, and giving. It's no wonder so many of us end up as people pleasers and struggle with the word no.

From the time I was 22, it felt like I was constantly asked to be in a wedding, go to a wedding, or attend a baby shower. I love my friends, and I love being there for them, but let's be honest, that shit can be exhausting and expensive. The first several of these events were super fun, and I was excited to be part of it and excited for the new experience. Then, friends started having second baby showers and even second weddings. Sometimes, it felt like I was spending my precious weekends doing things I'd rather send a gift for. I can't be alone in that, right? I promise I'm not a terrible person. I already know I'll probably get hate for this opinion, but baby showers and wedding showers are really not the epitome of fun. If wine is involved, though, or mimosas, it helps, still, I'd rather do something else. It's that they are always a Saturday or Sunday at 1 pm or 2 pm—middle of the day screwing everything up you want to accomplish (I realize I sound 87 years old here, but what can I say?). After a particularly busy summer of showers, I contemplated an invite to a baby shower of someone who was more of a peripheral friend than someone I kept regular contact with, and that was the first time I declined the invite and sent a gift. It was liberating.

Another life-changing moment with the word no is when I stopped feeling obligated to give a reason why I was saying no. It never occurred to me that a simple "I can't make it" would suffice, that they didn't in fact, need to know the full backstory. I would come up with the most detailed reasons to say no to try to soften the blow to other people, but really, it just made me feel selfish and like I was doing something wrong by saying no. I think this is the crux of it: we are inherently such people pleasers that we worry about disappointing other people by saying no, even when that's what we want to say. But disappointing ourselves is no better. In fact, it perpetuates the idea that we don't deserve to care for ourselves in the ways we need. It reduces our self-love tank.

People don't really care why you say no. You don't need to give them a full run down; you're not under oath or taking a lie detector test; it's your life, and you not attending something doesn't mean anything about the host. It simply says that you know yourself and love yourself so well you are honoring your needs, period.

After practicing this for a while, my friends began to understand my patterns and my needs. Pre-pandemic, I worked in outside sales, which meant I drove a lot and was out of the house most days from 7:15 am - 6 pm. I also was teaching multiple dance fitness classes throughout the week after work. By the time the week was ending, I was exhausted, and Friday nights became my "me" nights. I would either pick up takeout or something easy to cook. Have some wine, maybe do a face mask, and veg out on the couch in front of the TV. My friends knew that Dani was open Saturdays and Sundays, but only a very *rare* Friday night was I down to be social. They never took offense because they knew I needed this time, and it wasn't that I didn't want to see or spend time with them, but I am an outgoing introvert and needed alone, sloth time to recharge my batteries. Saying no is not a bad thing. It truly helps you get closer to yourself, and it sets important boundaries.

If it's not a fuck yes, then it's a no. Read that again. If it's not something that is a resounding fuck yes, it needs to be a no. This relates to all aspects of life. Look, I get there are things this can't 100% apply to: work, chores, eating broccoli.... they are all necessary, non-negotiables (for the most part, at least). What I'm talking about is all the other social events, work events, second dates, third dates.... you get the gist. If you don't want to say fuck yes I can't wait, then you probably should pass. One of my girlfriends and I were having this conversation one-day while walking, specifically about dating and this idea of fuck yes. In my romantic lifetime, I can tell you that there are several times it was absolutely not a fuck yes, and it should have been a hell no, yet I obliged nonetheless. Many of these instances are ones I am not proud of; many involved alcohol and looking to make other people happy more than me. As women, we're often conditioned by society that in heterosexual relations (my experience), the woman is supposed to please the man; this was my experience for way too many years. So many times, it wasn't a fuck yes, but I still was happy to please—I wish there was a pun intended. This never made me feel good. In fact, it made me feel empty and deeply unsatisfied. It surely never helped keep a man around as I thought it would, so it should always have been a hell no, and a fuck you.

Not long ago, I had gone on a few dates with a man who, on paper, was perfect: a business owner, gentleman, had his shit together, was communicative, handsome, it should have been easy. But on date three, after a mini-make-out session and groping on date two, he decided he would get a hotel for himself to visit me. We lived maybe 45 minutes away. At first, I appreciated his consideration in not assuming he could stay at my place, but then it was assumed I'd come to join him at the hotel—it was a resort. It all felt so forced, so unnatural. I pulled in to the resort, and the guard asked me for the name on the reservation. I gave the room number and they asked, what is the last name? I had no idea. So I texted him to get this information, already feeling like a goddamn call girl, only to then be asked if there was a different first name. There was. What the fuck? I could not relax. It felt so off and yet I felt weirdly obligated to be there. This man had paid for me to be at this resort-granted, it was down the street from my house, but he added me to the room and was paying for everything, I should have been enjoying this, should have appreciated this. Right? It was not a fuck yes. On the elevator ride down to the pool, we were alone in the elevator, and he, out of nowhere, pinned me against the wall and stuck his tongue down my throat. It was not hot for me. There have been times that would have been so fucking hot, but again, with him, it was never a fuck yes, so it felt odd and forced. The day went on, and we went back to his room to have wine on the patio. I knew what the upcoming sequence of events was going to be, and honestly, I just wanted to bail. Things started to escalate, and I could not shake the feeling in my body. It was visceral, screaming at me to get the fuck out of there and to remove myself from this situation. Part of me thought, what is the harm of just seeing it through, just get it over with? Maybe it will be fun; maybe I'll at least get an orgasm. Thankfully, a bigger part of me knew there was no way I could just sleep with this man out of some bizarre sense of obligation, orgasm or not. As a woman, I know I'm not alone in this experience. No part of these scenarios is acceptable, but they happen. We live in a weird society where we feel like we are obligated to please men, yet I knew that if I stayed in that room to please that man, I would be betraying myself. It was one of the most uncomfortable experiences of my life—I'm thankful that man didn't take advantage of me because the situation could have been WAY worse. I was very much indisposed, and he stopped to start asking questions about my recent relationships, etc. I was thankful that it was the day before Father's Day, and I was in my feels about that. But, I was also in my feels about this other man who acted like my boyfriend for months, only to gaslight me about his lack of commitment after I caught him on a trip with another woman, oh, and this all happened the day after I had an amazing first date with another man I really liked. I ended up in this hotel room with this man the same week as all this other shit....my emotions were a shit show, but maybe I was also a bit of a shit show.

Nonetheless, I told this man I was in my head, it wasn't him, it was me—he was so cocky he even said, "Oh, I know you are attracted to me"— but that I couldn't do this and wanted to leave. I put my clothes on and got the fuck out of there.

If it is not a **FUCK YES**, it's a **NO.**

There is a major cost when we say yes, even though our entire being is screaming no. It eats away at our soul, our being, our self-worth. Obligation is not a reason to say yes. Repeat that. OBLIGATION IS NOT A YES. I get it, friend, and you're going to upset people, maybe disappoint, perhaps even piss people off. Suppose you're someone with very minimal boundaries. In that case, folks are going to be confused AF that you're saying no, you're not showing up for them, or fulfilling your obligations, but that is part of the growth. That is the basis of self-love. Accepting the fact you may unintentionally upset other people by choosing yourself. Such is life. If you're a people pleaser, this is going to be excruciating. But I promise, this is how you move forward. This is how you show yourself the ultimate act of self-love. If this makes you cringe, well, go back up to my story and imagine it's your daughter, your friend, or your family member who is in a situation where they feel obligated to have sex with someone. Would you want them to go through with that even though they feel in their core it's a no? If so, then why would you want someone to show up out of obligation if they don't want to? I'm not suggesting you blow off everyone and everything in your life. I'm simply saying that if it's not a fuck yes, then it's a no.

Here are my top tips when it comes to NO:

1. *Listen to your gut.*

Your body knows the answer, but most of the time, we don't listen. Just like my story of feeling a visceral response to the situation with the man I was seeing, your body knows best. LISTEN TO IT! I can't tell you the number of times I've met people and had this feeling of "Nah, they are not good people," but yet felt like I was being judgmental. So I would ride it out, only to be shown that they were in fact, not good people. If you listen to your gut, it guides you.

2. *If you dread it, walk away.*

Look, I'm not saying walk away from caring for your children or your job (without a backup plan), but if you are dreading a coffee date, don't go. If you break out in hives in preparation for a party hosted by someone you really don't like, fucking stay home. Not all people deserve your time, and you deserve to preserve your energy. Walk the fuck away if you're dreading something because it's clearly a hell no.

3.   *Stop prioritizing other people's feelings over your own.*

We've covered this in some respects, but you cannot truly show yourself love if you're prioritizing someone else's needs over your own. Friends, family, and colleagues may be initially bummed you're saying no to their event, but if they can't understand your needs, you need to let it go. You'll never make everyone happy, so ensure you are happy first, and everything else will fall into place.

Section III:
The Life-changing art of gratitude, plus other practices to improve your life

Chapter 11
Cultivating a gratitude practice and writing shit down

When I initially began on my journey of self-discovery, it felt like every podcast, every self-help guru, and every influencer was touting how life-changing having a gratitude practice was to overall wellness. Personally, it felt like a "woo-woo" bullshit thing to do. Nonetheless, after some time, I thought, what do I have to lose? If it's good enough for Oprah, it's gotta be good enough for me. To say it was a rough start is putting it lightly. At first, I would just say in my mind something I was grateful for without any semblance of order. It didn't stick. Next, I tried to open the notes app on my phone and type something I was grateful for. It worked better than me saying thoughts in my brain, but yet it still didn't give me the results I imagined Oprah and all her friends were having. What was this life-changing magic, and how did I find it?

Naturally, like any human in this century, I opened the Amazon app on my phone and typed "gratitude journal" into the search bar. Let me tell you, there are A LOT of options. Ultimately, I settled on a day/night gratitude journal and was excited to give this "real" practice a go. I wish I had some out-of-body experience kinda moment I could share with you in vivid detail, but in reality, it wasn't like that. First of all, I could not get the evening reflection habit started to save my life, so I basically wasted half the journal. The morning gratitude started with the most superficial and, in my critical opinion, completely banal items. Could it have been any more obvious that a gratitude journal was needed, given I was critiquing each entry, expecting my list to be insightful and life-changing as if I were Ghandi? Cultivating this practice, though, was not as easy as I had thought it would be. Some days, it was a struggle to find anything I could truly say I was grateful for. On those days, I would find the simplest thing, perhaps my morning coffee. A warm home in the winter. The calm and quiet of the early morning. To be fair, these seemingly simple things are still, years later, things I truly am grateful for; the simplest things are sometimes the most beautiful.

There is nothing better than a quiet early morning, the calmness and peacefulness with that hot coffee, all curled up under a cozy blanket—that is perfection, y'all. Since I moved to Florida, I have liked to take my practice outside, basking in the beautiful weather and nature's beauty, yet another thing I'm overwhelmingly grateful for.

I'm sure you're thinking, wow, Dani, this sounds cute and all, but how did any of this actually change your life? I'm getting there, don't worry. When I found out my dad was diagnosed with Alzheimer's, I was not ready to accept it. He wasn't showing many signs yet, and I blissfully ignored it, avoided it, swept it under the rug, and put all those feelings in a box to the left, (to the left) in the closet, never to be visited again. Then, the disease began progressing, and the signs were too obvious to ignore. A piece of my heart broke and re-broke again every time I saw him. I was angry.

Compound this deep anger and grief with all the other superficial shit I was dealing with at the time, and I thought the world was against me. My mentality was that of a victim, and I did nothing to help myself. I ran away from anything resembling feeling by drinking, eating, binging shows, sleeping, going on dates with men I wasn't even really interested in, you name it. I couldn't have found my way to gratitude with a tour guide. My mindset was such that everyone had it easier than me in all aspects of my life. Someone had more money than me, had a husband, had a family, and found all that so easily while I was over here single, paying all the bills myself. This person didn't have to repay student loans because their parents were rich, and now they have bought a home, and I'm worried about paying rent. People at work had a better sales territory than me, and they made more money than me. I was a fucking nightmare. I was sick of my shit, and this is when the gratitude business began. It wasn't overnight that I felt the change, but gradually, though, that seemingly little practice slowly began to shift my entire being.

My dad's Alzheimer's diagnosis crushed me, and yet, it also saved me, as you're probably starting to gather. Let me explain. In my early 20's, I was a selfish brat. I used to get my feelings hurt way too easily, took everything personally, played the victim, and allowed other people's actions to stress me out, bum me out, and ruin my day. I hadn't grown up a lot, and I sweated ALL the small things (true care, truth brings). While I don't think you have to experience death, or even hardships to grow, I do believe that setbacks force you to gain perspective as long as you allow it. Much like hitting rock bottom, you can allow those devastating experiences to not only bring you back to reality and what is important in life but also grow into the best version of yourself. I didn't allow myself to gain this perspective for a while. I partied and avoided like the best of them, believing that if I acted as if it didn't exist, it would just go away. Clearly, life doesn't work that way.

A few years into my dad's diagnosis is when I began the gratitude practice, and as I've already mentioned, I felt like the world was out to get me. No way could anyone understand what I was going through. I was watching my dad slowly slip away in front of my eyes. In those early days, my practice consisted mostly of me saying I was grateful for my coffee in the morning, my dance fitness classes, my warm home, and Layla (my sweet dog). I didn't really feel grateful, though. I kept with the practice, almost every morning. Most days, it felt like I was simply going through the motions, but with time, a shift happened inside of me. I stopped believing the world was out to get me, instead, I began adopting the mentality that life is happening *FOR* me, and you know, it really was.

Here's what happens when you combine a parental death sentence with a gratitude practice: you are forced to grow, even if you're kicking and screaming the whole way through. Gratitude comes easily when you can acknowledge how fragile and short life is. I watched my dad be completely bedridden for 3 years. Honestly, I still don't know how that happened. He was mobile, albeit slightly unhinged one week, and then after having to endure a week or two long evaluation and med detox, he was prone in a bed since. Seeing my dad, the man whom I would play vigorous rounds of 1 on 1 basketball with—he did NOT let me win and did, in fact, play full out— or the same man who played baseball, jumped off our roof into the swimming pool, and would race my brother and I in running, swimming or literally compete on anything, become immobile; well to say it changed my entire life is an understatement. When I was feeling lazy and lethargic, preferring to stay in bed versus getting up for a workout, I would think of my dad and how he would —if in full mental and physical capacity—want to get up and move. This made me feel grateful that my body was mobile. Think about it. No, I mean, really think about it. There are SO many people in this world who would give anything to be able to walk, and yet we are so lazy at times we simply choose to stay perpendicular on the couch, avoiding any general movement. This simple idea alone changed my life. Anytime I wanted to be lazy or felt negative towards my body, I would think of my dad, and be reminded of how precious life is and be overwhelmed with gratitude for my body and its ability to move.

This feeling and mentality bled over into all aspects of my life. Frustrating situations at work, or annoying people in general; I would think that they are probably going through quite a tough time too and receive them with empathy and understanding. I would bless and release people and situations in a way that previously would have set me off. It became so much easier to remind myself, and truly believe, that if you won't remember the instance in five minutes, five days, or five months, then there is no reason to let it affect your present moment. Believe me, this mentality did NOT come overnight, nor do I think it was a given outcome because of my dad's illness. Pushing through the gratitude practice, even when I felt like it was superficial and pointless, is what created that outcome. Daily consistency through the fucking trenches of grief and pain generated authentic gratitude.

How do you start your practice? Pen to paper. Yes, old school. Grab an old notebook, write the date on top, and write: I am grateful for (blank). Once you can get that into practice for a week or two, add another item that you are grateful for. In a month, work up to three things you are grateful for. It will slowly become a habit after consistently writing these few sentences, and I bet you will look forward to spending that time each day. Now, if you want to take it up a bit, I suggest heading to Amazon and searching for a gratitude journal. I have two options I have used religiously and love both. The first journal was where I started my practice, and it is called "Gratitude: A Day and Night Reflection Journal (90 days)" by Inner World. This is a 90-day journal that gives you prompts for both morning and evening reflections. I used this exact journal for probably 5 years off and on, and it is tried and true!

Now, the second option is a little self-promotion. You see, I became the gratitude gifter, sharing my favorite journal with my friends as gifts so they could start their own practice. After gifting it to my friend Jordan and her using it consistently, we had conversations about things we loved in the journal and things we wished we could change (we still struggled with the evening reflection, but desperately wanted to be evening gratitude girlies). Eventually, we got our asses in gear and published our own gratitude journal! We poured our heart into it to give ourselves what we needed and hoped that along the way, we would inspire others to kickstart their practice. If you'd like to check that version out, it is on Amazon: "Unleashing My Power: A Woman's Empowerment and Gratitude Journal" By Jordan D 'Nelle and Danielle Begley. If you check either out, send me a DM or an email, and let me know your thoughts!

Continuing with the idea of writing shit down, free write in a journal. Take yourself back to adolescence, you probably had the super fun and adorable diary—maybe with a lock on it—and fun pens, and you'd write your innermost secrets, or maybe gushed about your crushes, or vented about a friend who was annoying you. If it had been a particularly angsty kinda day at school, you'd run into your room, blast some emo music, grab your diary, and let it all flow out onto the pages in hot pink or purple ink. Through the words, there may be a little crying session or furiously writing out your frustration until you run out of ink, but inevitably, once you closed and locked that bad boy up and shoved it back into its hiding place, you would feel better, lighter. I can seriously feel that faux fur fuzzy diary and gel pens in my hand right now, can't you?

When was the last time you wrote out your feelings? Facebook and Twitter do not count; those are like public rant sessions and not what we're trying to do here. It had been YEARS since I had an actual journal, and I am someone who wrote in a diary constantly. I even took little notebooks with me when I studied abroad in college and would write about my adventures and my experiences, the highs and the lows. Those are gifts for myself because I actually kept them (I'm known to throw a lot of things out for the sake of clutter), and I LOVE being able to read through those memories. I used journaling at that time to write about being homesick. To write about feeling out of place, or feeling like I found new friends, or when I felt like I was finding myself in a way I had never experienced. Journaling is like internal therapy, and it can be revolutionary.

I've been building consistency around journaling and aspiring to write free every day, a minimum of one page. One single page, in a small journal—not the college-ruled notebooks that would probably be like 4 journal pages, one single page. Somedays, it's weird, I think, "What the fuck do I have to say?". But when you allow yourself to just let the pen guide you, you'll be surprised at what the words are saying. For example, I have been writing about dating and my experiences. After some time of feeling like what I was writing sounded redundant, I paged back to sift through past thoughts and discovered patterns. Staring at me on multiple pages was my damn ego and issues around self-worth. Both were making regular appearances talking about these men, whom I didn't even believe were the right men for me—because I more than once would say exactly that in my journal, I had proof. Writing these feelings down and being able to have the space to reflect, allowed me to see the entire picture and make shifts. I was no longer stuck in the replay loop because the thoughts were out of my body.

Another instance was recognizing that the majority of the week, I would complain about my job; that was always the negative part of my evening reflection (when I actually got into that habit). This was eye-opening and the catalyst for me to begin searching for something new. Once I discovered the source of negativity in my life was stemming from my job, and I shared my desires for my next job with the universe, a'la writing it in my journal and speaking it out loud to friends, a new career entered into my life unexpectedly. It all unfolded in the most seamless and intentional way that could only be described as universe-guided. This is what can happen when you write shit down. You learn about yourself. Sure, you spend all day with yourself, but how much of that are you actually self-reflecting? I know folks who NEVER self-reflect and wonder why their life isn't how they'd hope. When you write things on paper, you are poised to discover new ideas and new feelings, and if nothing else, get them out of your head and onto paper. It's much like at the end of yoga practice; you leave it all on the mat and in the room; we're leaving all the bullshit and bad vibes on the paper and out of our bodies.

This is where growth can happen, and this is where our lives can change infinitely for the better. All it takes is a little pen to paper every day—you can write one page. This is not a dissertation; this is a single fucking page. I triple-dog dare you to try this for a week and then reflect on how it went. In my own humble opinion, there is no possible way this practice can make anything worse; it can only be a positive increase (or meh neutral experience), and in that case, fine, you wasted 7 pages of writing; at least you didn't have to read a boring book and write a report on it.

Listen, I know this sounds like such an easy practice, and it is! I assure you it will shift your perspective and outlook in the most positive way. Start small, stay consistent, and watch how you grow.

Here are the top lessons I've learned from writing it down:

1. *Don't sweat the small stuff—if it won't matter in 5 years, don't give it 5 minutes.*

Jerk cuts you off in traffic, tailgates you, cuts in front of you to steal a parking spot (I know driving really used to have me in a chokehold), you're not going to remember any of this in 5 days, 5 weeks, 5 months or 5 years. Be annoyed for a moment, and then let it go. It's so insignificant in the grand scheme of things. Bad hair day, pants are too tight, your dog poops on the carpet, and in the middle of the night, while walking to the bathroom half asleep, you step barefoot in it (has happened to me, and I don't recommend it)….. it's not going to be something pivotal in your life in the future, so bless and release it. Too many of us sweat all the small stuff. We allow instances out of our control to ruin our days, and for what? Life is too short. Save your big reactions for things that actually matter.

2. *There is always something to be grateful for.*

My dad's Alzheimer's diagnosis was not something I initially was grateful for, but it taught me many of these lessons I'm sharing with you. Without this horrible lesson and losing far too many loved ones early in my life, I'm not sure I would have gotten where I am today.

I'm not saying be happy about these situations because they are shitty, but I am saying that these things are not in your control, so find some kind of lesson and find a path towards some level of gratitude. It helps release the anger in your heart.

3. Life happens for you, not to you.

A victim mentality believes that life happens to you. They were so mean to me, they didn't like me and that's why I didn't get the job, or life is so hard, I can't ever catch a break. This is the victim mentality, and believing life happens to you does no one any good. This mentality is giving all the power up to things outside of your control while believing that life happens for you, allows you to take accountability for learning the lessons, and allows you to take charge of your emotions and your life. If we believe this, we can more easily find gratitude and have positive vibrations so that the universe knows we're primed to receive blessings because life is happening FOR US.

4. *Most things you can't control, but you can control your reaction.*

This tie's back to tip one because, let me tell you, I was Road Rage Reba, wooohhhhheeeee. I would scream and have the most intense reactions, and all it did was piss me off, probably jack up my blood pressure and have me arriving to work already feeling like I'd run a marathon before I walked in the door. No one can control traffic, so what the fuck is the point of getting pissed off? I started taking deep breaths and reminding myself that I'm on my way to work; I didn't even want to be there most days, so why am I trying to NASCAR race people to get there? Another lesson in this is how annoyed I would get that people handled situations differently than me. I would expect people to act like I would, and all it did was leave me disappointed. If someone decides to bail on you last minute, let them. If they are rude to you, fuck them, but let them. These situations all tell more about the other person and not you. Control what you can control and let them do what they're going to do

5. Rejection is redirection - let the door close, another one will open.

This one has been hard to learn, but it has brought me such peace. Relationships I thought would be "the one," or at least something special that ultimately turned out in heartbreak, would feel like such rejection, but in hindsight, I realized that it set me up for something better, or it protected me from a bad situation. In almost every failed relationship I've had I can look at it now and realize why it didn't work out and be grateful the rejection redirected me. When you're disappointed and feeling rejected, simply remind yourself that you are being redirected to something more beautiful, more special, and more fitting.

Chapter 12

Move ya body, girl... (make the fellas go)

I already know what you are thinking; great, just like everyone else in the world, Dani is telling me to fucking exercise. I know I was that way for a long time, but just stay with me for a bit, please? I grew up an active child and teenager. I tried every form of dance class and every sport our community offered, and even in the summers, once I started playing sports in junior high and early high school, I still stayed active in the gym, lifting weights or begrudgingly running. Once I left the sports world of high school, however, I had no reason to move, and I didn't. I went through phases in college where I'd go to the gym, mostly out of punishment, but I LOATHED being there. Needless to say, it never developed into a daily routine. You see, I always lived life with the idea that the only point of exercise was to make your body smaller, and I viewed it as punishment for when I ate too much or ate "badly," or simply the necessary requirement to lose weight, which as we've already learned, was the end goal most of my life. For me, exercise equaled punishment and obligation, which made me hate it.

I'm going to let you in on my secret—find some way to move your body that you actually enjoy. Some of you will hate that advice, but I truly do believe there is something out there for everyone, something that doesn't feel like medieval torture. As we've already talked about in earlier chapters, even people who like to exercise don't always wake up ready to get after it; they just know they will feel better. After YEARS of moving my body in ways I hated so badly, I would have to hype myself up for so fucking long to actually do anything that resembled exercise, so believe me, I get you if you hate exercise.

Want to know what I hate doing? Running. I don't get how people enjoy running. Does the runner's high *actually* exist, or is it some fantasy you imagine so you have something to strive for? For years, I tried to like it. So many people claim to love running, they actually love going outside and running down the damn road, and there are so many of them out there that they can't all be crazy. I'm convinced I'll never understand it, and I'm okay with it. I grew up idolizing the bodies of women who were super thin and fit, and they all seemingly were part of the running cult, so I figured I had to follow suit. Despite the fact I played basketball growing up, where running was part of practice, I always hated it. Maybe the liners as punishment during practice had something to do with my disdain for running, or maybe the fact I felt like I needed three sports bras so my tits would not bounce up and hit me in the face. Maybe it's the fact that a four minute song I absolutely love and gets me hyped feels like it's been slowed down to snail speed as soon as I start breaking into a jog. Or is that just me? All I know is that I tortured myself for years trying to get out there and run. If I didn't hate myself through running, I would hate myself with some other form of cardio, like the elliptical machine, where I would torture myself for hours in a way that was only slightly more enjoyable than jogging. No wonder I hated exercise.

Thankfully, during college, I was introduced to Zumba. It was my soulmate workout. Something I NEVER thought I'd say. Me, actually loving to workout? Who is this imposter person? I was studying Spanish in college, and I was obsessed with Latin music. It helped me learn the language and also it was just such a good vibe. Zumba, if you've never tried it, is an hour of cardio—but its dancing. There may be some squats or other forms of strength training, but mostly, it's shaking what your mama gave you to a bomb-ass music soundtrack. Even if you don't understand what they are saying (might be a good thing sometimes) the rhythm is something you can feel vibrate through your body. If I'm lying, then how is it that my mom, who does not understand Spanish, has had the Calle 13 song

Atrévete-Te-Te as her ringtone for YEARS?! She resonates with the vibe of the song, and that is what Zumba did for me. The even cooler thing is that taking Zumba opened the door to dance fitness and more importantly, the idea of group fitness classes—the community aspect that mimicked the camaraderie I had growing up playing sports. Most importantly, it showed me there was a form of cardio that did not feel like fucking torture. FINALLY! Can I get an amen?

I became obsessed with Zumba and was taking three classes a week. I began feeling more energetic and looked forward to that post-workout feeling (maybe the runner's high *does* exist after all). It took some time, but I started wanting to find additional ways of exercise, but for some reason the gym still intimidated me. Enter my era of Beachbody. It was not love at first sight like Zumba. I was torturing myself with the program Insanity, and the only thing that got me through those workouts was Shaun T's inspiring coaching because, as the name suggested, that workout was INSANITY. I dipped my toes into a beginner strength training program, which I really loved (21 Day Fix for all the now BODI folks). Lifting weights made me feel so strong. I went through this program for a round or two and ultimately decided to go big, and I began a program that was entirely focused on heavy lifting —Body Beast. This forever changed my relationship with strength training. I became a morning, before work, exerciser. Yep—one of those crazies. I still can't believe it either. Slowly but surely, I fell more and more in love with how strength training made me feel; waking up early before the sun rose, blasting my favorite music, and pushing myself to increase the weight left me feeling like such a bad ass. For a year at least, I built up my dumbbell collection, so much so that my beautiful mama treated me to a weight rack for my birthday. This obsession was not one of my phases, thank God. In fact, I toted that damn weight rack and all its dumbbells with me to Florida and hated myself for not selling it as I carried that collection of weights up three flights of stairs—talk about a workout. I've evolved from following Beachbody workouts to creating my own circuits. Sometimes, I still dive back into workout apps because, you probably know by now, I can get bored and want to switch it up sometimes. I don't believe you have to work out for hours and hours; honestly, for me, finding consistency came through simplifying workouts and getting it done in around 30 minutes. Finding a form of movement you can semi-enjoy, as well as fit into your schedule, is how it becomes sustainable and eventually your lifestyle. It becomes something you do, and you'll start feeling differently when you don't move your body. There may be times I only get a couple of workouts in a week, but I truly can't tell you the last time I went a whole week without some kind of movement—even on vacation (I know you're rolling your eyes, even I sometimes think who the F is this version of Dani?) because this is a lifestyle, not a fad—and more importantly, I know how beneficial the 20-30 minutes is to my mental health. It is therapy, period.

The second part of my secret is mindset. For so long, as I have already shared, I viewed exercise as torture, punishment, and required in order to make my body smaller. It wasn't for overall health, mental clarity, stress relief, or feeling good—only for the intention of changing my body. Exercise was a chore, something I HAD to do, nothing I ever wanted to do, a necessary evil. I've already mentioned that through my dad's battle with Alzheimer's, I began to witness his declining body. As he transitioned into in-home Hospice care, I wanted to give back and began volunteering to visit Hospice patients. Visiting nursing homes was a shock to my senses in that the majority of the patients needed help completing activities of daily living. Folks were unable to walk without a walker or a wheelchair. Dependent on nurses to get in and out of bed, help to go to the bathroom, to be fed. The fact I was even capable of moving my body became an absolute fucking blessing that I was reminded of every single time I stepped into one of these facilities. What people in these situations would not give for the ability to walk down the hall or get out of bed themselves, and here I am complaining about having to exercise—it sounds pretty pathetic.

Have you ever been injured and unable to move? Talk about annoying; you will very quickly realize how much of a gift the ability to walk with ease is in the midst of an injury. Is it nice to have some days where you lay in bed doing nothing or become the couch? Absolutely, I can sloth with the best of them. But what if you had no other choice but to stay in bed or on the couch? The novelty would wear off real quick. This idea is how I reshaped my mindset with exercise. It no longer was something I HAD to do or another annoying task to mark off the 'to do' list, it was truly something I GOT to do. Sounds easy, sure, but this simple shift is life-changing and can be applied to any aspect of your life. If you truly think that anything you "have to do" is a chore, a task, or an obligation, it doesn't sound like something that you would otherwise choose to do if you had any other choice. On the other hand, "getting to do" something sounds like a privilege, fun and exciting. I got to visit Paris sounds like a privilege, doesn't it? I have to feed my cat sounds like a chore. Flip the script. What a privilege it is to have a cute cat companion; why would feeding it be a chore? Simple word shift that yields immense impact.

My top tips for loving (ok, tolerating) exercise:

1.   *Try different varieties.*

There is more to the world than running and even lifting weights. Try yoga, cycling, swimming, any kind of group fitness class, martial arts, try it all. Also don't forget walking, that is moving your body and perfectly fine-especially for women! At some point, you will find something tolerable, and that can likely turn into a routine. You don't have to do dance fitness because I love it or yoga because your friend Caitlin is obsessed; do something you can semi-enjoy. Think outside of the box and find your soul mate exercise, or at least, your tolerable form of movement.

2.   *Find an accountability friend.*

Here is one of the coolest parts of group fitness classes—you can meet new friends! I met one of my absolute best friends, Emily, through Zumba. We bonded over a shared love of dance fitness, then overall health and wellness, and as we became closer, we realized how similar we were and she has become an integral part of my life. Through teaching group fitness classes, I've met some amazing people, including one of my other besties and travel partners, Jordan. If she hadn't put herself out there to try a class, and I wouldn't have put myself out there by teaching one, we would have missed out on an incredible friendship. These are the people I end up exercising with on vacations, trying new classes or trainings, and ones I can always lean on if I need accountability. You cannot underestimate the support that is having an accountability partner—they keep you honest and motivate you, and you ultimately don't want to disappoint them by bailing. You can bail and quit on yourself SO much easier than someone who is counting on you. Link arms with someone and get after it. Also, group fitness classes have been a godsend to me as I've moved to a new state and am trying to make friends as an adult. Shared interests through exercise is a great way to start.

3. *Check your mindset.*

If you wake up and nearly convince yourself to ditcht being active that day because you're tired or you don't feel like it, remind yourself of the bedridden people who are dependent on someone to get through the day and would give *anything* to be able to walk. You GET to move your body, and you don't have to. It's a fucking privilege that so many of us throw in the goddamn garbage on a daily basis, and if I sound pissed, it's because I am. It chaps my ass. So when I can't get my shit together, I channel that energy, and I'll tell you it takes about 5 minutes before I realize I'm being a privileged, lazy asshole and get my mind dand body moving. Your mindset is the answer—luckily, you get to choose it, so choose wisely.

Chapter 13
Personal development and the art of cultivating a morning routine

For most of my adult life, I would set multiple alarms to wake me up. The first alarm would normally start ten minutes before I'd like to get out of bed because I knew myself and I'd inevitably hit snooze, so then alarm number two would sound at the time I'd actually like to wake up. But then I'd have a backup alarm for 15 minutes after that. Another 15 minutes after that, and another--you guessed it--15 minutes after that. A zillion alarms alternated by 15 minutes all the way until the fail-safe alarm that gave me the bare minimum amount of time to get up, get my shit together, and get out the door. Without fail, nearly daily, I'd hit snooze until that final alarm buzzed, rushing around to get ready and leave for work; I'd be stressed, feeling like I'd run a marathon before I even walked into the office. With a thirty-minute commute (without traffic), I started feeling like by the time I got home in the evening, made dinner, and cleaned up, it was nearly time to get up and do it all over again. This is when I began trying to become a person who works out in the morning. I'm sure you can guess how successful that was in the beginning; knowing my snoozing through alarm tendencies, let's just say it took a while, but as you know, I'm one of the early morning exercisers now.

During this time of life, I kept hearing about this thing called personal development and how great it was. I had always been a bookworm, so I figured I'd give it a try. I remember the very first book I read back then, "You Are a Bad Ass" by Jen Sincero. This is still one of my absolute favorite books to this day and my most recommended to newbies in the personal development world. As someone who has read all their life, I wasn't yet convinced that this new practice would be life-changing, but I figured it couldn't make my life any worse. What I love about personal development is that it gives you a different viewpoint. I don't know about you, but I can get in my head and become very narrow-minded, and it's hard to see the big picture, an alternative picture, or anything else besides the 4 x 4 picture of my mind. Personal development is like a silent therapy session. It's food for your brain and mindset in such a different way than fiction reading is. Fiction, for me, is such an absolute pleasure, and I love getting lost in the plot, but it's for fun, like watching a movie or series on Netflix. Personal development is about growth and knowledge seeking, which is not something we as a society are customarily pursuing post-schooling. What I learned about myself with personal development is that spending a short amount of time on this daily set me up for a more productive tone for the day. Much like making my bed, reading personal development made me feel like I had accomplished at least one thing, even if the rest of the day went to shit.

Here is something weird you don't know about me, and I'm hoping I'm not alone in this, but I like certain layouts of books—the presentation matters to me. I like a book where the chapters are less than 20 pages because, let's be real, you can feel pretty accomplished reading 3 chapters as opposed to one chapter that's 40 pages, unless we're talking James Patterson books because unless he's changed his style, his chapters are like 5 pages max (why yes I've read 10 chapters). I also like spread-out margins—before you ask, I don't wear glasses, and I'm under 40; it's just aesthetic. Blame it on reading classical novels in high school, where the book was small enough to fit in a cross-body purse, but they jam-packed words onto pages as if it were prime real estate and made me want to go cross-eyed almost immediately. I am even like this at work—a PowerPoint full of words, an email that's a short story, a PDF that is in 8-point font, single-spaced, and I need to blow it up to 175% to read; my kind of hell. Am I alone in this? Please tell me I'm not the only one with a book aesthetic preference or a presentation aesthetic. Why the hell am I telling you this? It's because length, *ahem,* matters. (Get your head out of the gutter. I'm talking chapters ;))

Starting out on the personal development path can seem daunting if your goal is to read a chapter every morning, especially if that chapter is 30+ pages long. I completely understand this struggle—I'm currently reading a book where each chapter is damn near 40 pages, and I'm STRUGGLING! It can feel even more challenging when you're adjusting to waking up early—long chapters can consume even more precious time. You're likely to resort to speed reading, skimming, and feeling anxious about how long it's taking to finish the chapter compared to how much time you have left before getting ready. Ultimately, you retain nothing—defeating the purpose. Here's how I suggest starting: read 10 pages every morning. That sounds doable, right? 10 pages shouldn't take an eternity to read—unless the book layout is like those teeny tiny classic books I read in high school, but maybe that's your preference. 10 pages really isn't much, and you can easily turn it into a habit. It's a S.M.A.R.T. Goal—Specific, Measurable, Attainable, Realistic, and Timely. It's akin to training for a marathon or starting an exercise routine after being sedentary for a long time. You don't all of a sudden decide to kick things off by hitting the gym for 2 hours every day or running 10 miles on day one. If you do, I guarantee you will never keep up the momentum. I've been there—as we've already discussed when I decided I'm going to lose 100 lbs and cut everything out all at once—it is unattainable and torturous, and therefore, you cast it aside quickly. But when you start with 10 pages (or even 5), you can not only maintain that pace, but you will even begin to enjoy that pace. Personal development or self-help books are great, but it's not like reading a thriller where you just *have* to know what happens and stay up reading until the wee hours of the morning to find out who the killer is. No, these books are much easier to put down and start back up in the morning. The goal is not to read as many books as possible; it's about the idea of feeding your brain nutritional goodness daily. We consume a LOT of negativities each and every day and it's up to us to find good brain food to counteract all the BS.

So, what kind of books should you start with? Well, for me, I started searching "Top personal development books for women." I'd read a few synopses until something spoke to me. Maybe you're super into health, religion, or meditation, and a book of those genres speaks to you. Personally, now that it has become a habit, I enjoy switching it up. I've read books on money mindset, philosophy, words from monks like Thich Nhat Hanh, and books on love and relationships. I even read the Bhagavad Ghita. I've always been super curious- albeit too curious at times- I genuinely love learning a little about a lot. Grab a library card and explore. Maybe you even want to grab a group of friends and take turns swapping books. Honestly, the world is your oyster; see what you like, and you may surprise yourself. If reading is not your jam, then find an audiobook or a podcast that can also FEED YOUR MIND, (and the rest will follow). But if you go the audio version route, I would encourage you to find space to do so without multi-tasking on other things. Focus on the words as you listen, grab a notebook perhaps to jot notes down, and enjoy.

Reading personal development has helped and continues to help strengthen my mindset. It teaches me skills and tangible lessons to implement into my life. Having the 10 pages in the morning sets me up for success, further feeding my brain in a positive way, to which I will always be in support.

This is why cultivating a morning routine is life-changing. You don't have to follow mine; find your own, but find one. For me, once I began implementing a morning routine, I found I was calmer throughout the day. It took longer for me to get annoyed in traffic or roll my eyes at an email, and generally, my overall mood and mindset just improved. Again, it didn't happen overnight, but with consistency and over time, I started to feel a shift in the right direction. Now, the thought of even considering starting my morning by hopping out of bed and racing to get ready gives me a slight twinge of anxiety.

Once I finally got better at *actually* getting up earlier, it became easier to habit stack. I learned about this concept while reading "Atomic Habits" by James Clear (I definitely recommend this as a great PD book). He taught this concept, which truly changed my morning routine. The idea is that once you have one habit that you're consistent with, add another on top of it. For example, if I'm waking up early to write in my gratitude journal, I add reading 10 pages of personal development after. It makes it easier to build upon your existing habits and grow a practice this way. Rather than deciding to wake up 1.5 hours earlier tomorrow and cram in a workout, personal development reading, meditation, and gratitude practice, it's about building it over time, which allows things to actually become a habit. Here is how I did it. I started with a morning workout, then added a gratitude practice. Next, I added the personal development reading. From there, I added journaling (brain-dumping what was on my mind and heart) and meditating. Now, I'm super pleased with my routine and don't think there is anything else I want to add besides slowly extending my meditation practice. In total, the morning routine (without the workout) takes maybe 30 minutes. When you're cultivating your morning routine, make it a VIBE. Light your favorite candle, get cozy, maybe grab your coffee or tea, have nice mood lighting, and ENJOY. A morning routine can be so absolutely pleasurable, and I encourage you to find that pleasure!

But WHY is a morning routine so important? Well, it not only sets the tone for your morning, but your entire day, and it sets you up for success from the jump. It gives your morning a layer of zen. When you're not rushing around, you are not elevating your cortisol, and you can actually *enjoy* your morning calmly. Cultivating this routine truly changed mornings for me. I *never* thought I was a morning person, but now I am. There is something absolutely magical about the quiet and calm in the morning. When the majority of the world is still sleeping, it is slow, peaceful, and quiet, and it makes it even easier to quiet the mind since the world is so quiet. This brings such bliss into my life, and I believe this is why it's so crucial. If it were an afternoon routine, I don't think it would be as successful. At that point, you've already had half a day of "to-do's" and things you still have to do post-afternoon routine; it's hard to let your mind just be present. But first thing in the morning, you can be present as nothing has yet hijacked your whole day. Besides, the routine provides your day with an intention, much like a yoga practice: a focus, a guidepost, and an idea of which you are in complete control. Don't believe me? Google morning routine, and I GUARANTEE you will see thousands of posts from uber-successful folks who swear by their morning routines. It's time for YOU, period. It's honoring your needs and taking care of yourself. It doesn't need to be 5 hours, 2 hours, or even an hour. It simply needs to be a short window of time that is solely dedicated to you and your well-being. As I said earlier, it can't hurt your life, so what do you have to lose?

My Top tips to getting started with personal development and a morning routine:

1. Pick your personal development.

When I had a long commute, I started this journey with podcasts and audiobooks. I was already driving, may as well feed my brain, right? I'm all for this, assuming you can be focused. I've tried this practice while cleaning, working out, or putting away laundry and have noticed I really don't digest it as well. It's a step in the right direction though, and I think you'll still see the benefits. Pick something that works for you! If you're a busy parent juggling work and home life and chauffeuring kids around to activities and you only have 30 minutes, by all means, exercise while listening to your PD to make it work for you. Just do something that fits into your schedule, and once that is a habit, you can build from there!

2. Stay off your phone.

Listen; this one is HARD! I have do-not-disturb set for sleeping hours through my morning routine, but I still, at times, find myself bypassing it to see notifications, check email, etc., and I'll tell you, my morning routine isn't nearly as effective, my morning isn't nearly as zen and my brain is not nearly as clear as I want if I open my damn phone first thing. Stay off your phone from when you wake up until you're done with your morning routine. This is going to allow you to stay present, stay in the moment, and not let any news, or any negativity derail your "you" time. Trust me, it's worth it.

3. *Start slow.*

Habit Stack, my friend. Pick one thing and get after it. If you try to do 85 things all at once, it's never going to stick; believe me, I've tried. If you try to multi-task everything, it's also not going to work because you're not going to digest anything. It's better to pick one thing for five minutes every morning that actually makes a difference than five things you rush through that do *nothing* except allow you to check off a "to-do list." Start small, get your groove, and build! It's not a sprint, it's a marathon, and you are worth it.

Chapter 14
BBBE
Boundaries and
Bad Bitch Energy

The old version of Dani is probably laughing at the fact that I'm giving advice on boundaries because she was the complete antithesis of someone who had boundaries. A recovering people-pleaser, a recovering worrier of people's opinions, a recovering individual who wanted to fit in and take up as little space as possible— that was Dani. Boundaries protect your inner peace, so if you lack boundaries, your inner peace is likely lacking. It's much like how we discussed earlier in "The Subtle Art of Saying No"; boundaries protect you. You don't establish boundaries to intentionally upset people, but ultimately, it's about not sacrificing your own peace to avoid upsetting someone else, or better said, not prioritizing someone else's feelings over your own.

In every aspect of our lives, we have implemented some kind of boundaries without recognizing so. Generally, you have a time at night when you try to go to bed, and you have an amount of money you spend monthly on variable expenses, days that you don't take on any other obligations; these have been programmed without recognizing, so how can we improve in the areas where our boundaries are non-existent, or severely lacking?

Work boundaries can be one of the hardest at times to instill, yet in my opinion, absolutely crucial. I feel like millennials really struggle with this, probably because we witnessed the generation before us work constantly, and it yielded success. We in turn, perpetuated the idea that career and financial success were dependent upon your work ethic and the amount of time invested into your career. That was not exactly the case for us older millennials as we entered the workforce in the age of the 2008 financial crisis, and even in our mid-late thirties, some 15 years later, we are living in an economy that has faced the massive cost of living increases, and we are seeing that, unlike the boomers, killing yourself at work doesn't always translate to massive financial or career success. Gen Z, witnessing this shift, is prioritizing well-being over the insane career obsession of climbing the corporate ladder and they are forging their own path, and I give them massive props! They are proving that there are, in fact, ways to have massive financial success outside of the 9-5, and I am here for it!

Let's talk about the typical 9-5 and why boundaries are important. When I was working in outside sales, I had a slight chip on my shoulder—feeling like I had to be the best, prove that VP wrong that didn't want to hire me, sell as much as possible, and show how damn good I was. My ego was running the show, and as such, I essentially lacked any semblance of boundaries. My manager emailed me at 8 pm; of course, I would respond. Stay at the office until 6:30 pm, then take home more work to finish after dinner, no problem. Clients were emailing and calling me after hours or on vacation—no worries, I'll take care of it! I'm sure a lot of you are thinking, "Yo, Dani, why?" I imagine there are a lot of other potentially boundary-less workaholics who are thinking, "That's normal." The biggest problem—besides the obvious lack of work/life balance—is that once you begin this habit, it never ends. You can't be the person who is always available, responding at all hours of the day, and then switch it off. Now, people have an expectation of how you work, that you are always available, and it's not nearly as easy to implement a boundary after the fact. At least, this is my experience—if you have that figured out, bravo. For me, it took leaving a job and affirming to myself that in my next job, I would no longer be available outside of work hours; I was determined to draw that line in the sand early! Well, I started a job that had a busy season (if you've ever been part of Medicare annual enrollment, you can empathize), and with meetings literally back to back starting at 8:30 am and ending at 6:30 pm, I either had to take work home with me to catch up, or fall so far behind I would inevitably have to work weekends or nights anyways. I sucked it up through the insane few months, literally having no semblance of a life, and then jumped right back to my boundary. I will tell you, though, that I hated not having control of my schedule, and the emotional demands of that job were too much for me to bear. Ultimately, I think it was the lack of boundaries I was able to set for myself that made me resentful and ultimately leave that job.

Thankfully, after a year, I began a new career with the flexibility of remote work and with an incredible boss. As long as you get your work done, he didn't care. I had never really experienced that level of autonomy—and I LOVED it. For the most part, I have maintained my boundaries of not working crazy hours, with the exception of an early or a late call to accommodate global clients and wild time zone differences, and on those days, I tend to either start later or end earlier. It has been a game-changer. Setting that boundary allows me to maintain it, and if I decide I want to help future Dani out by getting through a few emails while waiting at the airport or in the back of my Uber, then it's fine—but I'm no longer feeling the stress, anxiety, and obligation to do so.

We spend a *huge* majority of our lives working, and in most cases, it's not as if we make any more money by working longer hours. Even if you do, at what point is the sacrifice of your life worth that cost? We aren't guaranteed any length of time on this earth. Tomorrow could be our last day. Would you really be happy looking back, realizing that you missed out on life, knowing your family and friends were all traveling and experiencing beautiful moments, and you missed it all for the sake of work? You can love your work and love your life; you don't have to work 80 hours a week to prove this. If you're efficient with your time, you can be a great worker, as well as actually live a life worth enjoying. I've seen people wait to enjoy life once they retire, only to then not be able to because of health reasons. I don't know about you, but I'm not going to waste my life away waiting until my late 60's to actually experience it. The crazy thing is that most of us working in traditional employment situations are replaceable. You may have a great "work family," but don't think for a moment that they wouldn't replace you in a second if they had to for the sake of the bottom line. It's nothing personal, but working for someone else should not be so personal, either. Having greater loyalty to your employer than your own life, for what? So you can die and have written on your headstone, here lies an amazing employee? No thanks. You may think I'm a typical millennial and have no loyalty, but I've got receipts as to why being a loyal employee that will give up my personal time does not get you ahead. Why else is it that, for a lot of workers, it takes getting a new job offer to actually get an adequate salary increase?

Boundaries have also come up in my dating life. Yep, you knew this was coming. For a while, it was almost as if when a man showed interest in me, I pursued it. I was content that they liked me; I didn't even question if I actually liked them. That led to a LOT of issues. I put up with more bullshit than I EVER in my life should have. Set boundaries in dating and your relationships. I don't care if you grew up believing that women should be nice and that we are here to please men. We've established that is fucking bullshit.

I have been the "chill girl" for most of my life with men, thinking (naively) that if I was easy to deal with and made his life easier and happier, everything would end up happily ever after. Nah, that's not how it works. You end up doing wifey shit for a man who will cheat on you or leave you for another woman. I wish someone would have taught me this earlier, or I could have figured it out earlier, and that's why I'm sharing this, we don't gatekeep around here. While I am single as I'm writing this book, it's by choice; it's not from a lack of interest from men, but it's from me not being willing to settle for less than I deserve. I'm not suggesting you be difficult or anything of the sort; however, I am absolutely suggesting that you prioritize yourself first, and this goes for women AND men. If a situation makes you unhappy, insecure, or feeling unsure—rectify it or move the hell on. Accepting the bare minimum and breadcrumbing is unacceptable. One of my boundaries now is that if a man cannot make a fucking plan to meet for a first date, I'm over it. I have been in my masculine energy for far too long; the assertive one scheduling dates and making plans, but if I can't get any reciprocal initiative to want to see me, why am I making such a huge effort, or any effort really? If someone wants you in their life, they will make time. I will absolutely make an effort to make plans with someone I want to see, but once that energy is not reciprocated, I don't want to do it anymore. Dating should be reciprocal, like a rubber band where both sides are under tension being pulled towards the effort. If only one side is making an effort to pull the rubber band, the other side is just being dragged along; that's not a place you want to be, period.

Not having boundaries = tolerating a bunch of bullshit.

It is really that simple. If you don't have boundaries, you will put up with so much nonsense you may not even realize it. I've been there, and I'm not calling you out, friend. We've all been at one point thinking, "I can change him," or "But he treats me so amazing sometimes," "He's just been busy," or " I know he cares about me, he just……" Once you start making excuses for the bullshit, you've got to realize it's on you. Everyone has bad days; everyone says things at times they wish they hadn't, but a real one will admit fault and apologize. If you're in a situation where the same shit happens every day, and you put up with it, you've got nobody to blame but yourself because you're accepting and tolerating the BS. Sure, would it be nice if everyone followed the golden rule and treated others how they wanted to be treated? Ugh, yeah, that would be amazing. But newsflash, it doesn't work that way. People are selfish. They can suck, and let's face it, sometimes a man (or a woman) just wants access to you without commitment, and they will find ways to give you the bare minimum or tell you what you want to hear to keep that access, even though they *know* they aren't planning to make any real commitment to you. If you allow it, they will continue. For example, I always have wondered why men think it's a great idea to send a woman an unsolicited dick pic or to immediately be sexual in talking to someone new, and what I've realized is that its clearly worked at some point in their lives, or else they would never do it. That's the boundary for me. If someone I barely know starts going sexual, I call them out on it. When you are confident in yourself, channeled into your bad bitch energy, and have boundaries, you no longer tolerate this level of bullshit. You don't have time for it, and your energy is too precious to be shared with someone who would treat you that way.

This leads me into bad $bitch energy. Bad bitch energy is a feeling. It is about embodying the amazingness, the uniqueness, the sassy, the badassery, and the incredibleness that is you. It's walking through life carrying yourself, knowing how fucking amazing you are. It's not playing small, not shrinking, or trying to take up less space. It's flooding the room with your energy. You have seen those people who walk through a room and command it; that is BBE, baby! Bad bitch energy exudes confidence, and as you can imagine, it was not something I possessed most of my life. I'd say the type of energy I exuded was more akin to scared bitch energy or desperate to be small bitch energy. I thought the only women in the world who were confident were supermodels, actresses, and thin, commercially beautiful women. I could not imagine a world in which a plus-size woman could be confident, and that is how I carried myself. Baggy shirts, long shirts, skin covered, shoulders hunched over, walking with my eyes down, trying not to be noticed. When I began working on building my confidence, I felt a shift. Slowly, I was stepping into that bad bitch energy and carrying myself as so. I have proved to myself that confidence is sexy and attractive. I've been thinner, and I've been heavier, and regardless of my size, I now carry myself with confidence, and it doesn't matter my weight; men approach me. I'm stopped by women to be told how beautiful I am, too, and it's mad. Listen, I'm not trying to sound conceited. I'm only trying to prove a point. I've been a size 12, all the way up to a size 22, and have had men attracted to me all the same. Your size doesn't fucking matter, but your confidence does!

A confident bad bitch does not settle for an inconsistent partner, who makes her feel anxious, who makes her question herself or feel bad about herself. She doesn't tolerate bullshit. Now, scared bitches tolerate the **BS** because, in their minds, they don't feel worthy of more, they aren't confident in themselves, and they're willing to settle for the bare minimum as opposed to being alone. I was that girl for a while, and I was miserable—I lost myself, and it showed. I've been single for a long time. I've dated, and dated, and dated, but the difference is, I'm not settling for someone who makes me anxious, questions my worth, or completely de-regulates my nervous system, and because of this ideology, I'm still single—I'm okay with that. I believe that there is a healed, amazing man out there who will love me and my **BBE**.

Bad bitch energy isn't only applicable to romantic relationships, but it is also relative to work and goals. Bad bitches don't allow themselves to be taken advantage of, they stand up for themselves at work, they don't play small, and they get shit done. You can be nice, but you can be assertive too. I've learned this about myself. I don't have to be a bitch to show I'm serious, I can be nice and bubbly, which is my actual personality and innate nature, but I'm not afraid to be assertive when needed. That is a bad bitch.

BBE is pursuing your goals and passions with enthusiasm. I've been a lazy waste of space often. But something clicks in me when I'm going after a goal, much like writing this book, and I won't let anyone get in my way. A couple of years ago, I was fed up. I was reading books constantly, and I simply felt a pull in my heart, "I could do this." Sure, I had no formal training in writing, publishing, or editing, and it had been years since I'd actually paid attention to grammar and the structure of writing, but I knew in my soul that if so many people in the world could do it, I could too. Besides, simply finishing the book was more important to me than anything else. As long as I finished, it didn't matter if anyone else read it. I was achieving this goal for me. That is bad bitch energy. It's a vibe. It lives inside us all, but it's up to us to decide to embody the energy. I promise when you do, your life will forever be changed for the better. Now, let me see that BBE, baby!

My top tips to instill boundaries, be a bad bitch, and stop the bullshit:

1. *Notice what robs you of your true self and set a boundary.*

Whether it's dating, a family member, a friend, a job, or an obligation, if you constantly feel like you are changing yourself, shrinking, or ending up feeling depleted; insert a boundary here. A friend that only brings negativity? Stop giving them your time. I get it if you're a people pleaser. I've been there. You don't have to cut them out of your life if you don't want to, but maybe stop spending as much time with them. Limit the exposure with a boundary. Boundaries may ruffle some feathers, but remember, setting a boundary protects YOUR PEACE. It's not for the other person, and ultimately you're either making their lives better,or your own; choose wisely.

2. *WWABBD?*

When in doubt, ask yourself, "What would a bad bitch do?" Give a loser 6 months of your life and let them treat you like crap? A bad bitch would never. Let your work nemesis take credit for your idea? NEVER! Tell someone they're "just fine" when really they are upset? Not in this lifetime. I'm telling you, when in doubt, ask yourself if this is something a bad bitch would do and proceed accordingly. We ain't playing small, my friends!

3.   *Stop putting up with bullshit.*

Active boundaries mean no bullshit. This is the moral of this chapter—STOP PUTTING UP WITH THE BULLSHIT GIRL! I swear if I could go back in time and calculate how much time I've wasted dealing with the bullshit I allowed into my life, I'd be so embarrassed. What does putting up with bullshit teach you? That someone else's feelings are more important than yours. That you'd rather suck it up for them than deal with it for yourself. The longer we perpetuate that idea, the longer we live in inner turmoil. There can be no peace in an environment thriving on negativity and bullshit. It all ends here. When you feel like you're being treated badly, being taken advantage of, or it feels like a sham, walk the fuck out. We don't have time to put up with bullshit.

Chapter 15
When all else fails, breathe.

Sitting still in silence for extended periods sounds kinda like torture in the modern world; no phone, no TV, nothing to pass the time but you and your beautifully wild thoughts. At first, if it's been a long day, it feels like heaven, settling into the quiet and calm, and then the thoughts start racing. "Should I be breathing this fast?" "What am I going to do this weekend?" "OMG, I still can't believe that I made out with Chris in 10th grade. I wonder what he is up to now; I need to remember to check his IG" "8675309, 8675309," "Who sings that song? Did they have any other hits, or were they a one-hit wonder?" "How am I feeling hungry again?" "I kind of need to pee." OMG, BRAIN, SHUT UP! "Inhale, exhale, inhale 2, 3, 4, exhale 2, 3, 4." Welcome to a front-row seat into my brain, and I would guess a lot of your brains, too. We are constantly on the go, thinking, thinking, planning, thinking, thinking, all day, every second, every minute, every hour, of every fucking day. When we have a silent moment, we fill it with more ideas, more questions, and more information from our phones or the TV; anything but our actual thoughts. I'd say we all are overdue for a few deep, calming breaths and some meditation. I've read a book on meditation and have taken in-person meditation exercises, hell I'm a licensed yoga instructor, and yet my brain still, at times, has the exact racing and jumbled thoughts as above. No, I didn't just do a line or pop an addy; my thoughts are nonsensical like that sometimes, and it is evidence of just how desperately I need meditation.

Meditation is one of those things that is so simple, its difficult. Much like the idea of playing golf seems like the easiest thing in the world, you're telling me I grab a club and hit this ball towards the hole in the ground, and that's it? Easy peasy. WRONG. Golf is stupid hard, and it's frustrating because it's so simple, its hard, just like meditation. I'm not going to pretend I'm a golfer; I'm not. Maybe one day, but honestly, I get bored—9 holes max for me; also, I can't drive the ball for shit.

Golfing experience aside, do you think that when Tiger Woods walks up to the tee, his brain is going 100mph, thoughts ping-ponging around between 175 different things? Hell no. He is focused on the task at hand. His breathing is relaxed; nothing else in the world exists besides him, his club, the ball, and the hole. If he has a bad drive, he re-focuses on the next drive and isn't thinking of the last hole, onward and upward. This is meditation. It is a quiet, centered, and focused moment. If your brain starts braining and your thoughts wander back to the Pythagorean theorem and why on earth you needed to learn that, you simply shift back to your breath, your body, and your peace and leave the geometry back in high school.

The world we live in is high-stress, and most of the time, our cortisol levels are constantly on edge; while we can't control everything, we can control our breath and our focus, and for me, this is why I love meditation. The idea is that you can always come back to your breath to calm down and that connecting your body and breath can bring you back to the present moment, even if your anxiety is racing towards the what-ifs of the future or back to the WTFs of the past. It is a beautiful FREE medicine. I'm still learning, practicing and growing, all while continuously trying to get my thoughts to kindly zip it, but daily intentional breath is absolutely something I recommend. I set a timer for 5 minutes minimum and focus on my breath, the natural rise and fall of my belly. Focusing on shutting out racing thoughts and being present. Meditation can be spiritually awakening-thoughts, ideas, and clarity can come into your mind that you may NEVER have thought while your brain was busy in overactive mode. In fact, the idea for this very book came into my mind one day during meditation. Pretty rad, huh? Try a couple of minutes of meditation and see how you feel. I love doing this in the morning before the stress of the day. Some people love it at night before bed to wind down and come back into the body. Whatever feels best for you, give it a try and breathe.

Why the importance of breath, Dani? Well, I'll tell you, anxiety. The word 'anxiety' gets thrown around a lot in our modern world: social anxiety, test anxiety, anxious attachment; the list is endless. Humans manage a LOT; whether we manage it particularly well all the time is debatable. But we are in a constant state of "doing" and not a lot of "being." Even when we allow ourselves to be, it's difficult not to feel anxiety or guilt creeping in because we believe we're wasting time if we're not actively "doing." I think this can be a big part of anxiety. At least for me, it has been. Wanna know how I handled anxiety and emotions for the longest time? Over-scheduling myself, so I'm so busy I have no time to think about my feelings, and by the time I finally have a moment without a commitment, I'm so physically and mentally exhausted I essentially sink into the couch and disappear into TV land. I very much am an outgoing introvert. I can be super bubbly and a social butterfly, but the only way I must recharge my batteries is by being alone. As I've mentioned, at one point in my life, I worked a full-time job with a 45-minute commute each way and was teaching 4 group fitness classes in my free time. I was constantly on the run, constantly having to be the biggest energy in the room for both the fitness classes AND my sales job, and by the time Friday rolled around, my gas tank was empty. I couldn't look forward to anything else besides ordering food and curling up on my couch sloth-style.

When COVID hit, and I wasn't teaching as many classes, I didn't know what to do with myself or my time. For a while, I felt lazy, unproductive, and useless. Having so much free time made me feel like there was something wrong with me or like I wasn't doing anything right, and it gave me anxiety. This belief stemmed from the idea that my worth was based on my productivity; productive = worthy, and unproductive = unworthy. I had to unpack that, and I still have to unpack that belief at times. Some of the best advice I've heard is that your brain has so many ideas and thoughts, but it is our choice to believe these ideas to be true. Or, we can decide to acknowledge them as simply thoughts and move on. Our brain simply has thoughts. It doesn't mean they are real or true. When we realize it is our choice what we believe to be true about ourselves and our beliefs, it removes the pressure and, for me, a lot of the anxiety.

The thing about me and my anxiety is that most of the time, if I can make myself remain present in the current moment, I can quell the anxiousness. This is why meditation, yoga and breath work have become pivotal pillars of my overall wellness routine—they all are practices to improve presence. When we are focused on the past, we can feel shame or guilt about what we've done and what we haven't done and think, "if only I would have done "x" differently." How does this serve you? IT DOESN'T! All it does is fill your brain with overactive thoughts on situations that have already happened, and that can never be changed. Focusing our time and investing our energy in past events not only discounts the beauty that is the current moment but it blocks good energy from being received. Learn from the past, grow from the past, and forgive yourself.

Similarly, if we're thinking about the future, what we have to do, what we need to do, what if this happens, what if, what if, what if…hello anxiety. We're freaking out so much over things that may or may not happen that we become paralyzed in our thoughts, anxiety rushes over us, and we're again stuck in our heads. The present moment is now. If we can stay in the present, we save ourselves from anxiety and overthinking and open ourselves up to experience the beauty of what naturally evolves.

As you know by now, my dating life has been an absolute dumpster fire at times, so why not bring up how anxiety has screwed me with dating, because I bet you can relate. Anxiety has NEVER helped, nor has the past or future overthinking, and I realized recently that is one of my problems with dating. I become so focused on the future what if's instead of just remaining focused on the present moment and letting things evolve. This year, I dated a guy that I thought at some point could actually be a guy I seriously dated.

He made me feel safe when I was with him. I felt taken care of and desired, and we laughed *a lot*. It was effortless when we were together. We had a good first date, lots of laughs, and I felt super comfortable with him (that doesn't happen all the time). Our second date was even better. We went to one of the immersive art experiences, made candles, and had an amazing dinner. I didn't want it to end. On the third date, we cooked dinner together, and he brought me flowers, wine, and even treats for my dog (who was this guy?). These instances clouded my judgment, and I ignored my intuition because I really liked spending time with this guy. When we were together, I felt calm, but when we were separated, I was an anxious fucking mess. This man lit up my anxious attachment style before I knew what that meant. For months, I felt riddled with anxiety, despite knowing deep down that this guy was not my guy, and yet I kept at it like I had lost all my intellect. He was inconsistent and arguably a terrible communicator, but even though he treated me like a girlfriend, at times had even called me his girlfriend, he said he wasn't ready for a relationship. WHAT? The problem was me falling for the future possibilities and not acknowledging the current moment for what it actually was—which was clearly him telling me exactly what I needed to hear (even though I didn't listen). Those first few dates, I felt something I hadn't in so long that I started thinking of how the future would be with him, the trips we'd take; I started planning in my head. WRONG MOVE. I also would re-read texts or replay past encounters to validate his feelings for me or decipher behavior. Not at any time was I staying in the present moment. I was either ruminating on the past or stuck in anxious overthinking. In hindsight, if I had stayed in the present moment during our time together, there is a huge chance I wouldn't have stayed around as long as I did because I would have fully been aware that he was not only not ready for a relationship, but that I deserved better. Since that short-lived romance, I have implemented a new approach to dating. If I find myself quickly focusing on a future with a person I don't know that well yet, I quickly bring myself back to the current moment. The other thing I no longer am here for is creating false intimacy in nonstop texting early in dating. I know myself and the temptations that my brain has to psychoanalyze behaviors, and if after a week or two of good morning texts or good night texts, if a day goes by without one, my brain goes completely into overdrive—all when I could honestly care less about a good morning or a good night text in the beginning. Managing my anxiety is more important, and truly, I believe that someone who is meant to be in my life will not make me feel like an anxious mess. This approach has truly brought me peace in dating, and I only wish past Dani knew this sooner.

Finding mindfulness is a lot easier when your energy is clear, which is more likely when your mind is clear, your space is clear, and overall, you're clear. Imagine it's early morning, the sun is rising;

the only sound is the low chirps of birds slowly awaking; it is peaceful and quiet. You glance around the room before you attempt to begin your meditation practice, and there are piles of clutter everywhere in sight. In fact, you just felt something poke into your leg, and you're noticing it's starting to smell musty in here; good luck clearing your mind. When your physical space is cluttered, so is your mind. Maybe it doesn't bother you, but after a few days of crap cluttering my space, I started to realize how it makes me annoyed, lazy, and overall just not centered. The longer my space is in disarray, the more I start feeling like an episode of hoarders, and my anxiety is never quelled. If you feel extra anxious and have been working on staying present in all aspects of your life and nothing seems to be working, take a REAL look around your space. Is shit crammed into every crack and crevice? Move one thing out of your cabinet and have to shield your head as cups and Tupperware are falling off their overcrowded shelves. Let's maybe take an hour at a time and do some purging and get shit organized. You don't need the Tupperware bowl with no lid; you can get rid of the cup that never looks clean because it's so old. Take it one area at a time, let go, and see how much lighter you feel. The clearer your space, the clearer your mind.

Tips for mindfulness and staying present:

1.   Set a timer for 60 seconds.

You can do anything for 60 seconds; set a timer and focus on breathing and calming your mind for 1 minute. Once this feels good, try for 3 minutes, then 5, then 7, then 10. Intentionally slowing down the mind will prepare you to handle stressful situations more calmly, it will lower stress hormones, and overall, you will feel zen. Personally, I would rather feel zen than stressed every day.

2.   Breathing techniques.

Breathe in for 3 seconds, hold for 3 seconds and exhale for 3 seconds. Make these breaths the biggest and deepest breaths you have ever taken in your life. Inhale so you can feel the breath come up through your belly to your chest to your throat and nose, and let it all out with an audible sigh. Getting the negative energy, the anxiety, and the bullshit out of your body will reset your system. Our nervous system holds in all this extra stress and anxiety; moving it out of your body releases it all. Even if you think I sound like a hippie, what do you have to lose?

3.   Pick up before bed.

Take 5 minutes and straighten up before bed. Most days, it's the last thing I want to do, but when I wake up, and my sink isn't full of dishes, and there isn't junk sitting all over my counter, I'm thankful I took a couple of minutes the night before. The procrastination of putting away a few things for me **ADDS UP!** It may start as a shirt on the floor, but before long, it is 10 pieces of clothes piled on the floor, in a chair, or anywhere else besides in my closet or drawer. Take a few minutes before bed to make your rounds, and start your day off with a clean space and mind.

So, what's next?
Let's keep it moving.

We didn't come this far just to come this far. Don't be someone who reads this book and doesn't apply a single thing. Believe me, I've done that, and it's not helping anyone. I appreciate your support in reading my words, but don't sell yourself short. My rationale for sharing some of the most painful parts of my life and how I used the pain to grow is to encourage others to do the same. Stop allowing your body, or anything else hold you back from the greatness you deserve and are worthy of. I hope this book can be a stepping stone for you, a toe dip into personal development and finding space to hold for yourself. Maybe it can be a catalyst for truly loving yourself and letting go of all the body baggage. Whatever this book does for you, I appreciate you, and let's keep moving forward, friend.

Without further ado, here are "Next Steps":

1. Start small.

We've discussed this already, but please do not decide to implement every single practice in this book all at once; that is a recipe for burnout and giving up. I love and appreciate the ambition, but this is not a sprint; it's a marathon that I want you to actually finish. Pick one practice that resonates with you the most to implement. After three to four weeks of consistency, look to habit stack another practice. Then after another three to four weeks of consistency with both practices, maybe add in another. For me, it takes about three weeks for habits to actually stick, which really helps build consistency over time. I know you want to feel great and change your life, but I promise small steps consistently over time will get you there, babe.

2. Know your fucking worth.

This is something I will forever be practicing and working through. Our worth is inherent within us. History, situations, and experiences have all shaped our beliefs about our worth—mostly subconsciously. It's not until we begin to unpack our baggage and truly dissect our thought patterns that we can understand where our issues lie. What does that look like? Well, for me, there have been times when I believed that a very attractive, successful, and healed man would never be interested in me. I chalked it up to low self-confidence, which was part of it, but truly, it was more about my worth. I believed that he wouldn't find me attractive because I was plus size, and I held onto that thought because society has conditioned us to believe that our value as women is based on our bodies, and ultimately, I felt unworthy. But my worth has nothing to do with my body. My worth is determined by how I show up for myself in this world, how I treat myself when no one is around, and how I treat others. It has everything to do with what I believe about myself. We are all worthy of our wildest dreams, but the problem is that we all have deep-rooted stories we've repeatedly told ourselves that make us doubt our worth. You have to believe you are worthy, or you will always settle for less. I've done that most of my life. All that does is make you play small, make you feel less than others, make you compare yourself and ultimately make you fucking miserable. So, if you are feeling like you're not deserving of something, take a minute to ask yourself why. Then, ask yourself why again and again until you get to the root of the issue. If that doesn't help, focus daily affirmations on your worthiness, "I am worthy of love." "I am worthy of abundant wealth." "I am worthy of loving myself." Check yourself. You are worthy, my love; don't let anyone—even yourself—make you feel less than.

3. Therapy and do your checkups.

Sometimes, the best medicine is talking it out with someone who doesn't know you. If you've never tried therapy, I highly recommend it. There are so many options nowadays, and not for nothing; I think the whole world would be a better place if we all had mandatory therapy. We are not built to understand how to process our emotions. If you didn't grow up in a home where emotions were healthily expressed, you easily could have learned coping mechanisms. Even if you did grow up in that type of environment, I am confident that along the way, you have developed some kind of coping mechanism. We all go through life biting our tongues, holding shit in, and inevitably we either fall apart at something completely ridiculous or blow up at something equally ridiculous— think about all the road rage in the world (I'm guilty, too) and tell me we don't all need to figure out how to process our shit. Therapy is like a checkup for our emotional well-being. Try it, and see. Speaking of check-ups, do your basic health check-ups. No one likes going to the dentist, or getting a pap smear or mammogram, but they are necessary in prevention. Besides, it's an act of treating your body like you actually give a shit about it. To love your body, you must take care of it, so do your checkups.

4.   Surround yourself with support.

Humans are hardwired for connection and community. This isn't a popularity contest or high school where we need to be surrounded by 20 people. I'm saying quality over quantity. Find a circle that supports you, encourages you and is there when you need an ear to listen to. It's okay if your family doesn't provide this; it's okay if you don't have this in a friend either, but find a supportive circle. I've found great support in the dance fitness community—people who genuinely care about you. If you don't have it, find it. Seek out a group that has similar interests as you do, or even create your own group—build it, and they will come. Again, you can start with therapy as well—that is support! Whatever you do, find some kind of support system to help you weather the storms that life sometimes brings.

5.   Make this one life count.

I must sound like a broken record by now, but in case you haven't picked it up yet, I'm ending the book on this concept. We have one life. ONE. We don't get to redo it, fast forward or rewind it. If we hit the pause button, time doesn't stop and wait for us to be ready. It keeps moving all around us. Our days are not guaranteed; they are limited and at an unknown amount. If you were told tomorrow you had six months left to live, how would you live differently? I hope you wouldn't sit around and feel sorry for yourself, but instead, actually, go DO the things you want to do and be around the people you want to be around. I know it's morbid to think about, but it's just a fact, my friends. If you were on your deathbed and reflecting on your life, do you have regrets? Do you have things you wanted to accomplish that you didn't? Places you wanted to visit? People you loved that you never told? Loved ones you never made amends with? I don't know about you, but I don't want to sit around and wait for life to happen to me. I want to be in the driver's seat and make shit happen. I've seen firsthand how short life can be. Our health is not guaranteed. Our ability to walk, move, see, hear, taste, feel— nothing is guaranteed. You can be loyal to your job, your family, your community—I'm not saying to stop caring about those things as long as you care about them. However, I am insisting that if there are deep rooted desires you have, what are you waiting for? Go after them, plan it, just do it. Stop the excuses. Forget what people may think about your choices; if it is in your heart, it's there for a reason. Do not waste this life. You are worthy. We need your contributions to this world. We need your energy when you're pursuing your purpose. We need your shine, so please, if you take nothing else from this book, shine bright like a diamond baby and enjoy life while you still can.

Acknowledgements

Whew, where do I even begin? This book has been a labor of love; it's been therapy. As a kid, I fell in love with books. Diving into a book, sailing away into an alternative universe and uncovering the story page by page has been a safe place for me. I have to thank my Grammy for being part of the reason I fell in love with books so young. I can vividly recall countless nights sleeping over and reading stories; it was love at first sight. To my Mom, who has always encouraged me to be true to myself, to chase my dreams and to believe in myself. You've always believed in me, even when I didn't believe in myself. You always see the best in me, even when I can't. I thank you for being an amazing inspiration, a steady guidepost, and never pressuring me to be anything other than me. I have found my strong voice and opinions, in thanks to you. I love you so much. Even though it annoyed me to no end as an obnoxious teen, your constant quoting of the Rolling Stones, "You Can't Always Get What You Want", I now wholeheartedly appreciate it because we can't always get what we want, but if we try sometimes, we get what we need. That's the universe, and it knows what we need.

Thanks to my tribe, my friends who have become family. I am constantly inspired by you all every day. You've allowed me to be vulnerable, forgiven me for my mistakes and encouraged and supported me in all aspects of my life. Thank you, Tara, Ashley,

Emily, Paola and Jordan, for being my chosen family and supporting me in writing this book since the very beginning. Thanks to my little Layla for being my best little furry friend and keeping me company while writing with your little snores and cuteness.

Thanks to everyone who has been part of my journey, who shaped me into who I am today, even all the men who got more press than I would like; for better or worse you taught me necessary lessons, and I appreciate you.

Thank you to my Dad, your love is something I carry with me every single day and I hope you look down at me from Heaven and are proud.

Thank you to my launch squad, who agreed to support me while on this journey of figuring out how to get my book into the world. I appreciate you for cheering me on, sharing your feedback and ultimately being an incredible support system to me! Some of you are family, childhood friends, past work friends, brand new Florida friends that have made me feel so welcomed in my new home, I appreciate you all! Thank you to Betsy, Debbie, Kim, Kristen, Lindsey, Liana, Gina, Katie, Erica, Jen, Nikia, Melissa, Jessica, Ashley, Beth Ann, Leslie, Sherrie, Angela, Ginger, Jennifer, Jordan, Isabella, Katie, Tara, Paola, Kylie, Emily, Adee and Stephanie!

Thank you Jane for reading, editing and formatting this book, I appreciate you so much!

Thank you, the beautiful person reading, for picking this book, for spending your time and money and reading my words. I was scared to share these parts of me and I am grateful for your warm reception.